~ *Entertaining* ~
# GLUTEN FREE

L POWER

COPYRIGHT © 2013 L POWER
ALL RIGHTS RESERVED.
ISBN-10: 1483946827
EAN-13: 9781483946825

Introduction

I love to cook and entertain for others. Setting the table and laying a good meal people can enjoy while sharing excellent conversation and company is, in my opinion, at the heart of most social occasions. You simply do not realize how integral food is to these social occasions until it becomes a barrier. Often, Celiacs, or Gluten Intolerant people, feel cut off from the entertaining value of meals; not just eating, but the meal aspect of families getting together and enjoying each other's company over good food.

When my son, who was four at the time, was diagnosed as a Celiac in 2010, I was at a loss as how create food that tasted good, was nourishing and not coming out of box. It became a passion to find and develop recipes and meals everyone, regardless of dietary restrictions would enjoy to eat. I wanted people to sit at my table and again enjoy the meal and not think, oh, this tastes 'different' because it's gluten free.

I am not a complicated cook, who has time, really? These are recipes that are straightforward, easy to find the ingredients and easy to assemble. I believe this cookbook will fill in the gap for those of us who love to cook without hassles.

The cookbook is broken into meal occasions instead of appetizer, main, desert, etc., as again, I feel it is important to keep things simple. *Entertaining Gluten Free* is formatted around those special family occasions where the whole menu is laid out with no flipping back and forth between trying to choose an appetizer, the salad and then the main course.

I hope you will enjoy assembling these meals as much as I have; Enjoy.

Table of Contents

1. **New Year's Feast** 1
   - BAKED BRIE WITH SWEET RED CHILE PEPPER ... 3
   - APPLE SOUP ... 3
   - BUTTER BASED BREAD ... 4
   - CHERRY GLAZED HAM ... 5
   - PINEAPPLE DRESSING ... 6
   - GARLIC MASHED POTATOES ... 7
   - ASPARAGUS ... 7
   - CHOCOLATE CHUNK BANANA CAKE ... 8

2. **Chinese New Year** 11
   - CHICKEN SALAD ... 13
   - WONTON SOUP GF STYLE ... 14
   - PINEAPPLE HONEY CHICKEN BALLS ... 15
   - MEAT BALLS ... 16
   - SWEET & SOUR SAUCE ... 17
   - PORK WITH CASHEWS ... 18
   - BROCCOLI SIR FRY ... 19
   - CHICKEN FRIED RICE ... 22
   - COCONUT CHERRY BALLS ... 23

3. Valentine's Day — 25

- Decadent Hot Chocolate — 27
- Sundried Tomato Soup — 28
- Tomato, Mozzarella & Basil — 30
- Savory Pork Roast with Apple Stuffing — 31
- Baked Potatoes Florentine — 32
- Roasted Winter Vegetables — 33
- Carrot Cake — 34

4. Family Day — 37

- Baked Stuffed Mushrooms — 39
- Caesar Salad — 40
- Egg Plant Lasagne — 42
- Garlic Toast — 44
- Cottage Pudding — 44

5. Hockey Night — 47

- Prosciutto Wrapped Peppers with Feta — 49
- Corn Bread — 50
- Texas Chili — 50
- Caramel Popcorn & Chocolate — 52

6. Groundhog Day — 53

- Hot Artichoke Dip — 55
- Sour Cream Pancakes — 56
- Spinach with Strawberries — 57
- Lasagne Wraps — 58
- Rice Pudding — 59

7. Zorba the Greek — 61
HUMMUS	63
GREEK SALAD	64
DONAIRS	65
SOUVLAKIA	66
TZATZIKI	67
GREEK HONEY PUFFS	68

8. Mardi Gras — 71
TOSSED SALAD WITH HONEY MUSTARD DRESSING	73
CRAB SOUP	74
BARBEQUED SHRIMP	74
CATFISH CASSEROLE	76
CHOCOLATE TRUFFLE CHEESECAKE BROWNIES	78

9. St. Patrick's Day — 81
DILL DIP	83
STEW	84
BOSTON CREAM PIE	86

10. Sink the Titanic — 89
BAKED ONIONS, FRENCHED	91
GRILLED TOMATO TUMMIES	92
HONEY-MINT FRUIT SALAD	92
GOAT CHEESE STUFFED MUSHROOM	93
CHICKEN LYONNAISE	94
ROASTED PORK LOIN WITH DIJON AND ROSEMARY	95
ROASTED MANGOES AND STAR ANISE	96
BAKED MINI POTATO GALETTES	97
ASPARAGUS WITH OKA	98
DECADENT TRUFFLES	99

11. Easter Lunch — 101
- Fruit Salad with Pineapple Dressing — 103
- Honey Berry Bread Pudding — 104
- GF Pie Crust — 105
- Spinach and Sweet Onion Quiche — 107
- French Onion Soup — 109
- Graham Wafer Cheese Desert — 110

12. May Day — 111
- Mixed Greens with Buttermilk Coconut Dressing — 113
- Beef Stroganoff — 114
- Fettuccini — 115
- Basic Cake — 116
- Frosting — 116

13. Cinco de Mayo — 117
- Fresh Salsa — 119
- Guacamole — 119
- 5 Layer Dip — 120
- Taco Salad — 120
- Salsa Chicken — 121
- Mexican Taco Steak — 121
- Spicy Rice — 122
- Strawberries and Chocolate — 122

14. Mother's Day — 123
- Baked Tomatoes — 125
- Asparagus Ham Rolls — 125
- Cream of Cold Carrot Soup — 126
- Beef Bourguignon — 127
- Chocolate Dainties — 128

15. Fun Friday — 131
- Baked Tacos — 133
- Chocolate Pudding — 134
- Party Mix — 134

16. Father's Day — 137
- Pork Skewers with Dipping Sauce — 139
- Corn and Red Pepper Chowder — 140
- Barbequed Beef — 141
- Spicy Fries with Dip — 142
- Apple Crisp — 143

17. Taste of the Maritimes — 145
- Cranberry Bread — 147
- Salmon Salad — 148
- Clam Chowder — 149
- Caramelized Scallops — 150
- Scallop Casserole — 150
- Blueberry Grunt — 152

18. Grading Day — 153
- Ice Cream Soda — 155
- Pizza Mix Appetizers — 156
- Cranberry Chops — 156
- Dressed Mashed Potatoes — 157
- Green Bean Casserole — 158
- Marshmallow Chocolate Squares — 158

19. Canada Day — 159

Lemonade	161
Picnic Salad	162
Barbeque Sauce	163
Steak Medallions	163
Potato Salad	164
Corn on the Cob	164
Onions in the Skin	165
Summer Breeze	165

20. Birthday — 167

Yogurt Pops	169
Marshmallow Fruit Kabobs	169
Pizza Crust	170
Pizza Sauce	170
Toppings	
Chocolate Cake	

21. Summer Barbeque — 175

Lemon Freeze	
Grilled Caesar Salad	177
Ribs	178
Baked potato	178
Sweet and sour onions	179
Strawberry Shortcake	180

22. Labour Day — 183

Stuffed Cherry Tomatoes	185
Strawberry salad with sweet and garlic dressing	186
Chicken Cordon Blue Salad	187
Potato Stack	188
Carrots and Cranberries	189
Acorn Squash	190
Banana Butterscotch	190

23. Sunday Dinner — 191
- Roasted Tomato and Chipotle Chicken Appetizer — 193
- Pot Roast — 194
- Potato Strata — 195
- Ginger Carrots — 196
- Braised Pearl Onions with Peas and Bacon — 196
- Cherry Cheesecake — 198

24. Chilly Day — 199
- Fruity Salad — 201
- Ham Chowder — 202
- Biscuits — 203
- Fairy Gingerbread — 204

25. Thanksgiving — 207
- Zucchini Salad — 209
- Cranberry Sauce — 210
- Turkey — 211
- Dressing — 212
- Gravy — 213
- Creamy Mashed Potatoes — 213
- Yam Pie — 214
- Green Beans — 214
- Turnip — 215
- Apple Cake — 216
- Caramel Sauce — 217

26. Halloween — 219
- Gutsy Burgers — 221
- Broken Fingers — 221
- Dirty Ghosts — 222
- Oozing Apple Lanterns — 222
- Brown Sugar Fudge — 223

27. Nice 'n Easy — 225
- Roasted Portabella Salad — 227
- Coconut Shrimp Curry — 228
- Coconut Ginger Rice — 229
- Chocolate Coconut Cookies

28. Football — 231
- Prosciutto wrapped Chicken — 233
- Buddy burgers — 233
- Potato wedges — 234
- Coconut coleslaw — 234
- Chocolate Chip Cookies — 235

29. Remembrance Day — 237
- Cranberry Spinach Salad — 239
- Biscuit Lips — 240
- Cinnamon Honey Butter — 241
- Sweet Chilli Pork Lettuce Wraps — 241
- Oven Baked Rice — 242
- Asparagus with Cashew Butter — 242
- Apple Strudel with Vanilla Sauce — 243

30. Company's Coming — 245

- Spinach Salad — 247
- Mulligatawny Soup — 248
- Maple Ginger Pork Chops — 249
- Parmesan Potatoes — 249
- Curried Carrots — 250
- Quick Pudding — 251

31. Christmas Eve — 253

- Spiced Apple Cider — 255
- Ham rolls — 255
- Sheppard's Pie — 256
- Gingerbread People — 257
- Shortbread Cookies — 258
- Christmas Cake — 259

32. Christmas Brunch — 261

- Land of Nod cinnamon rolls with cream cheese icing — 263
- Egg sandwiches — 264
- Omelette Casserole — 265
- Poached Fruit — 266

33. Boxing Day — 267

- Green Tea Latte — 269
- Stuffed Peppers — 269
- Turkey bake — 270
- Potato Delux — 270
- Squash and Apple Saute — 271
- Ice Cream with Chocolate Fudge Sauce — 272
- GF Rice Crispy Squares — 272

34. Dinner with the Mob — 273

- Sausage & Peppers — 275
- Roasted Peppers — 275
- Meatballs — 275
- Clemenza Sauce — 276
- Spaghetti — 276
- Pasta Fagiole — 277
- Sicilian Meatloaf — 278
- Custard Cream Gelato — 279

1.

New Year's Feast

Sometimes, it is just being pointed in the right direction. Not everything has gluten in it and there are so many 'regular' foods that can indeed be included in a meal, it is just a matter of knowing where to look.

Certainly when family or friends have us over for dinner, one of the first questions they ask is 'what can you eat?' Followed closely by, 'you can eat cheese?, you can eat meat?, you can have vegetables, right?'. Of course, but people are nervous and need a nudge in the right direction.

~ Menu ~

Baked Brie with Sweet Red Chile Pepper

Apple Soup

Butter Based Bread

Cherry Glazed Ham

Pineapple Dressing

Garlic Mashed Potatoes

Asparagus

Chocolate Chunk Banana Cake

BAKED BREA WITH SWEET RED CHILE PEPPER

Round of Brea cheese
Sweet red chilli pepper marmalade, ensure GF

~

Bake Brea in 350°F oven for 20-minutes in small round casserole dish just big enough to fit cheese. Remove cheese from oven, make small slices in cheese with sharp knife and cover with marmalade.

Serve hot with GF crackers

APPLE SOUP

4 c apple juice
4 apples, peeled, corded and diced
½ tsp cinnamon
1 tsp lemon juice
½ c brown sugar, packed
Cinnamon sticks (optional)

~

Simmer all ingredients together, covered in large pot until apples are barely tender. Chill and serve cold with cinnamon stick.

BUTTER BASED BREAD

<u>For bread machine</u>
2 c rice flour
½ c potato starch flour
½ c tapioca flour
⅔ c carnation instant milk
3 tsp xanthan gum
3 tbsp sugar
½ tsp salt (optional)
1 ⅔ c hot water
¼ c butter, melted
3 lg eggs room temperature
1 tsp vinegar
1 tbsp yeast

~

Take 1 c of hot water and add butter to melt.

Use ⅔ c hot water, add eggs and beat well, add 1 tbsp of sugar.

Place liquid ingredients in bread machine pan, add dry ingredients on top reserving 1 tbsp of sugar and yeast for very top of mixture.

CHERRY GLAZED HAM

    6 lb ham
    1 can cherry pie filling (checking ingredients to ensure GF)
    1 tbsp cider vinegar
    2 tsp prepared mustard
    Cloves

~

Cook ham in roaster according to weight, typically 2 ½ hours. The internal temperature should be 130°F to indicate doneness.

Stir remaining ingredients together in saucepan over medium heat until hot. Spoon ½ to 1 c over ham; brush sides to glaze. Cook uncovered in 350°F oven for 10-15-minutes until glaze is a bit dry. Slice and serve with remaining sauce around ham or on the side.

PINEAPPLE DRESSING

- 1 can pineapple chunks
- ½ c butter
- 3 tbsp brown sugar, firmly packed
- 7 c GF bread crumbs
- ¼ pecans, coarsely chopped
- ¼ raisins
- ¼ c cranberries

~

Drain pineapple and reserve juice, add water to juice to make 2 c liquid.

Place butter, sugar and juice in large saucepan and cook over medium heat, stirring occasionally until mixture begins to bubble. Remove from heat.

Add GF breadcrumbs all once, tossing to moisten. Add in pineapple, raisins, cranberries and pecans. Toss again to mix thoroughly. Spread evenly in greased 9x13" casserole dish.

Bake at 350°F for 25-minutes until heated through. Serve hot.

GARLIC MASHED POTATOES

    6-8 potatoes
    3 cloves garlic
    1 tsp dried dill
    ½ c sour cream
    1 tbsp cream cheese
    Dash salt & Pepper to taste

~

Peel and cube potatoes, place in large pot with water for cooking. Take cloves of garlic and smash to remove skin, add directly to water and potatoes and cook for 25-minutes, until potatoes are soft enough to run a fork through easily.

Drain potatoes in colander, put back in pot and mash adding in remaining ingredients and whip until smooth.

ASPARAGUS

    Bundle of asparagus
    2 tbsp butter
    ¼ tsp nutmeg

~

Add vegetable steamer to pot. Place ½ c water at bottom and bring to a boil. Add asparagus spears with the hard ends chopped off. Steam in boiling water for five minutes. Set timer and ensure no longer as asparagus will become limp.

When done, sprinkle with nutmeg and add butter to top to melt on its own.

CHOCOLATE CHUNK BANANA CAKE

⅓ c oil
¾ c water
1 c sugar
1 ¼ c rice flour
1 ½ tsp xanthan gum
1 ½ tsp soda
1 tsp cider
2 Aero chocolate bars (chunked) (optional)
3 frozen bananas (just thawed)
2 egg
½ tsp salt
2 tsp vanilla
Sprinkle cinnamon

<u>Topping</u>
1 tbsp brown sugar
2 tbsp whipping cream
1 Aero bar
1 tbsp butter
¾ c coconut

~

Can be made without the chocolate.

In large bowl, mix sugar and egg together until smooth. Add in oil and mix well. Add water, 1 c of rice flour, xanthan gum, salt and vanilla and mix until smooth. Dollop soda on top of mixture and pour cider directly on top of soda to create fizz, add in remaining rice flour and mix well.

Bananas thaw quickly if added to hot water for about five minutes. Add slightly thawed bananas t mixture, crumble the chocolate bar and sprinkle with cinnamon and mix well.

Spread evening in bunt pan and bake at 350°F for 40-minutes until knife inserted in middle comes out clean.

For the topping, in saucepan place heat chocolate bar, whipping cream, brown sugar and butter over medium heat until melted and smooth. Add in coconut and drizzle over cooled bunt and serve.

2.

Chinese New Year

When I first started dating my husband, his mother, who is a wonderful cook use to always have people over for a big Chinese meal – Canadian style. I wanted to continue her tradition by expanding it to Gluten-Free style.

~ Menu ~

Chicken Salad

Wonton Soup GF Style

Pineapple Honey Chicken Balls

Meat balls

Sweet & Sour Sauce

Pork with Cashews

Broccoli Sir Fry

Chicken Almond

Chicken Fried Rice

Coconut Cherry Balls

CHICKEN SALAD

    2 chicken breast, boneless, halved
    Water to cover
    <u>Dressing</u>
    2 tbsp vinegar
    3 tbsp sugar
    1 tsp oil
    ¼ tsp dry mustard
    1 tbsp GF soy sauce
    ¼ tsp onion powder
    <u>Salad</u>
    ½ tsp oil
    1 lg egg, fork beaten
    2 c bean sprouts
    2 c romaine lettuce
    2 green onions, chopped
    ~

Cook chicken in water in saucepan for about 18-minutes until there is no pink in middle and juices run clear. Drain, cool and cut into strips. Chill until ready to assemble salad.

<u>*Dressing*</u>

Combine all dressing ingredients together in mixer and blend until smooth and sugar is dissolved.

<u>*Salad*</u>

Cook egg in oil until set, turn to cutting surface, cool and cut into thin strips.

In large salad bowl, combine all salad ingredients and toss until mixed. Add dressing and toss to coat. Serve cold.

WONTON GLUTEN FREE STYLE

8 GF lasagne noodles, cooked to package directions
½ med bok choy
2 green onions, sliced
1 leek
4 med mushrooms, sliced
4 c GF chicken stock
2 tbsp GF soy sauce
½ c left over roast pork, cut in 2" slivers
8 c water

~

Cut green, leafy tops off bok choy and chop into small pieces. Cut white stalks into matchstick sized pieces. Put green and white silvers into large pot. Add green onion. Cut off bottom and top part of leek and discard. Cut white part in half crosswise. Sliver into matchsticks and add to pot. Add mushrooms and GF chicken stock. Bring to a boil. Cover and simmer for 20-minutes.

Cut GF lasagne noodles into 2" squares and reserve to just before serving, add to soup to heat to through about 5 minutes before serving.

PINEAPPLE HONEY CHICKEN BALLS

2 lbs fryer chicken, cut into bite sized pieces
1 tbsp ginger, minced
½ tsp garlic, minced
1 c pineapple chunks
1 green pepper, seeded and cut into 1" squares
1 carrot, sliced
4 green onions, cut into 1" lengths

<u>Sauce</u>
2 tbsp honey
2 tbsp GF soy sauce
1 tbsp cooking wine
1 ½ tbsp corn starch
⅓ c water

~

Fry chicken in small amount of oil until golden brown, remove to paper towel to drain excess grease.

With small amount of oil in wok or large frying pan add in remaining vegetables and cook until tender crisp.

Mix sauce ingredients together in separate bowl until blended smooth and pour over vegetables in wok until thick. Add in chicken and serve hot.

MEAT BALLS

    1 lb burger
    ¼ c water chestnut, chopped fine
    1 tsp sugar
    3 tsp GF soy sauce
    Dash pepper
    1 sm onion, chopped fine
    2 tbsp corn starch
    1 tsp ginger
    2 stalks green onion
    Chinese 5 spice
    ~

In large bowl, mix all ingredients together, form mixture into balls. Place on baking sheet and sprinkle with Chinese 5 spice. Cook in 350°F oven for 45-minutes until golden brown.

Serve with sweet and source sauce.

SWEET & SOUR SAUCE

    1 c water
    1 c pineapple chunks
    1 carrot, thinly sliced
    ⅓ c vinegar
    ¾ c sugar
    2 tbsp corn starch
    1 sm can tomato paste

~

In small container, mix cornstarch with ¼ c of water until smooth.

Bring remaining water to boil in pot, blend in sugar, vinegar and tomato paste. Once boiled, add in cornstarch mixture and blend until smooth and thickened. Reduce heat and add in carrots and pineapple chunks. Simmer for 10-minutes and then add in meat balls. Stir to coat.

Mix and serve hot.

PORK AND CASHEWS

4-6 boneless pork chops, cut into bite sized strips
1 tbsp corn starch
1 tbsp GF soy sauce
1 tbsp oil, divided
2 cloves garlic, minced
1 tsp ginger, minced
2 green peppers, diced
½ c unseasoned cashews
¼ c GF chicken stock

~

Combine pork, cornstarch and GF soy sauce, marinade for 15-minutes in fridge. Heat 1 ½ tsp oil in skillet and add in ginger and garlic to stir fry for 1-minute until fragrant. Add pork and continue to stir-fry until done, remove from pan.

Add in remaining oil and vegetables and stir-fry for 2 minutes before adding back in the pork and continue cooking an additional 2 minutes. Add in water and bring to a boil to thicken.

Spoon into platter and top with cashews.

BROCCOLI SIR FRY

1 c broccoli floweret's, chopped
¼ c red pepper, seeded and cut lengthwise
1 celery stalk, chopped
½ c carrots, cut into matchsticks
1 green onion sliced
1 ½ tsp lemon juice
1 ½ tsp GF soy sauce
2 tsp oil
~

Put oil into large wok or frying pan, heat to medium high heat and add in broccoli and remaining vegetables and cook until tender crisp. Add in lemon juice and GF soy sauce, stir to mix and serve hot.

CHICKEN ALMOND

    3 chicken breasts, halved
    1 lg onion, sliced
    1 tsp salt
    Dash pepper
    Water
    2 tbsp oil
    1 ½ c celery, chopped
    1 ¼ c peas, frozen
    1 can mushrooms, sliced
    1 tbsp cornstarch
    ½ tsp ginger
    2 tbsp GF soy sauce
    Uncoated slivered almonds

~

Combine chicken, 2 slices of onion, salt and pepper and 1 c water in large saucepan, cover and simmer for 20-minutes.

Remove chicken and set aside.

Strain broth; cut chicken into thin strips.

Saute remaining onion with oil in skillet until tender, 2-3-minutes, stir in celery and cook for 2-minutes, add peas and mushrooms with liquid, cook slightly, add in chicken slices and then the broth, cover and steam for 10-minutes.

Lift vegetables out of pan with slotted spoon, place in serving bowl. Lift out chicken and place on top.

In small bowl, blend GF soy sauce, cornstarch, ginger and 2 tbsp of water until smooth. Stir into broth mixture, stirring constantly until thickened and boils, about 3-minutes.

Spoon over chicken and vegetables, and sprinkle with almonds.

CHICKEN FRIED RICE

5 c cooked rice
½ cut broccoli
½ c cut cauliflower
½ c frozen peas
½ c fresh mushrooms
1 c cooked chicken, chopped
2 eggs
5 tbsp. GF soy sauce
3 tbsp rice wine vinegar
1 tsp minced ginger
1 tsp minced garlic
1 tsp sage
Olive oil to cook with

~

Using a wok or large frying pan, sauté all vegetables in olive oil until soft.

Make space in the middle, crack and cook eggs in empty space and scramble until cooked through. Mix with vegetables.

Add cooked chicken and spices to vegetable mix, combine thoroughly. Add cooked rice and stir vigorously to coat with vegetables, spices and chicken.

COCONUT CHERRY BALLS

½ c butter, melted
1 ½ c icing sugar
1 ½ c coconut
2 tbsp milk
1 bottle maraschino cherries, drained

~

Add icing sugar, coconut, and milk to melted butter, mix until thick like a pastry.

Mould mixture around each cherry and set on baking sheet lined with wax paper.

Place in fridge to cool. Serve cold.

3.

Valentine's Day

I will tell you true, no one in my house ever enjoyed out of the can tomato soup, so I was weary to try to make this from scratch. Where was the incentive, other than I always enjoyed restaurant quality tomato soup? I am pleased to say, it was an enormous hit! So much so that sometimes, just on a cold winter day, I will make the tomato soup with biscuits to satisfied sighs.

Now to the other standout in this line-up – the Carrot Cake – honest, I have requests for this cake! The prep, I will admit is a bit of time, but assembled correctly, is sure to please!

~ Menu ~

Decadent Hot Chocolate

Sundried Tomato Soup

Tomato, Mozzarella & Basil

Savory Pork Roast with Apple Stuffing

Baked Potatoes Florentine

Roasted Winter Vegetables

Carrot Cake

DECADENT HOT CHOCOLATE

    2 ½ c milk, divided
    1 c 18% table cream, divided
    ¼ c sugar
    ¼ c unsweetened cocoa powder
    Pinch salt
    1 tsp vanilla

~

In saucepan heat 2 c of milk and the cream over medium heat, stirring often until steaming.

Meanwhile in a bowl, whisk together sugar, cocoa and salt. Whisk in remaining ½ c of cold milk and vanilla to make a smooth paste.

Reduce heat to medium low and gradually whisk in cocoa mixture into hot milk mixture until blended. Heat stirring for about 2-minutes or until steaming hot. Ladle hot chocolate into mugs and serve immediately.

SUNDRIED TOMATO SOUP

    2 tbsp extra virgin olive oil
    1 c sliced onion
    4 med tomatoes, peeled, seeded and chopped (in a hurry? Use 2 cans of whole tomatoes)
    1 tsp sugar
    1 tbsp chopped fresh basil
    ½ tsp chopped garlic
    Pinch fresh or dried oregano
    1 bay leaf
    4 c chicken stock
    ⅓ c sundried tomatoes
    ½ c whipping cream
    Sea salt with fresh ground pepper

Heat olive oil and gently sauté onion until tender.

Blanch tomato in boiling water, transfer to cold water, then peel, seed and chop when cool. Add tomato and onion, cook 5 minutes until softened. Add sugar, basil, garlic, oregano and bay leaf. Cook a few minutes longer, stirring often.

Pour in chicken stock, bring to a boil, and then reduce to a simmer. If using dehydrated sundried tomatoes, blanch sundried tomatoes in boiling water for 30 seconds and strain. If using sundried tomatoes packed in oil, remove from oil and pat dry with paper towel.

Add half sundried tomatoes to the chicken stock and reserve the rest for garnish. Let soup reduce by a third, remove bay leaf and puree mixture in food processor or blender. Return to saucepan, bring to a simmer and stir in cream.

If soup us too thick, thin with water or stock. Chop remaining sundried tomatoes in small pieces and add to soup. Season with salt and pepper if needed.

TOMATO, MOZZARELLA & BASIL

    6 large lettuce leaves
    6 sm tomatoes
    1 lb fresh mozzarella
    2 tbsp basil pesto
    2 tbsp olive oil
    Salt & pepper

~

Arrange lettuce leaves on serving plate.

Slice tomatoes and mozzarella and arrange on lettuce leaves.

Mix basil pesto and oil together and drizzle over the top.

Sprinkle with salt and pepper to taste.

SAVORY PORK ROAST WITH APPLE STUFFING

2 garlic cloves, minced
1 ½ tsp rosemary
1 tsp sage
¼ tsp black pepper
2 c med apples (2 apples), peeled, cored and sliced
½ c celery, chopped
⅓ c onion, chopped
6 c GF bread crumbs
1 c apple juice
¼ c butter
1 tsp salt
1 boneless rolled pork loin roast (2 ½ - 3 lbs)

~

Preheat oven to 350°F.

In small bowl, mix garlic, rosemary, sage and pepper. Remove ½ tsp of this mixture and set aside for stuffing.

Mix apples, celery and onion in a large bowl. Add in GF bread crumbs, apple juice, butter and the ½ tsp of prepared seasoning. Toss and spoon into deep casserole dish.

Add salt to seasoning mixture and rub over pork roast.

Place roast, fat side up, on top of stuffing mixture, cover and bake for 1 ½ hours, remove lid and continue to cook an additional 30 minutes until internal temperature registers 155°F.

Let stand covered, 10 minutes before carving.

BAKED POTATOES FLORENTINE

    6 baking potatoes
    1 pkg frozen spinach, thawed, drained and cut
    ¼ c butter
    ⅓ c onion, finely chopped
    ½ c mushrooms, finely chopped
    1 tsp salt
    ½ tsp rosemary
    ¼ tsp pepper
    ½ c sour cream
    ½ c real mayonnaise
    <u>Topping</u>
    2 tbsp butter
    ½ c green onion, chopped fine
    ½ c bacon bits
    ½ c cheddar cheese, grated fine
    ~

Scrub potatoes, prick with fork and bake in 400°F oven until done, 45-55-minutes.

While potatoes are cooking, drain as much moisture off spinach as possible, chop fine and set aside.

In large saucepan, melt butter over medium heat, cook onions for 2 minutes, stir in mushrooms, salt, rosemary and pepper and cook for 3-4-minutes until vegetables are tender. Remove from heat, add in spinach, mix thoroughly and set aside.

Once potatoes are cooked, cut a slice from the top of each potato, scoop out the insides into a large mixing bowl, leaving ¼" thick shell. Mash potato and stir in spinach mixture, sour cream and mayonnaise. Spoon mixture back into potato shell and smooth top.

Place on platter and put back in oven to cook an additional 10-minutes until heated through. Serve with toppings.

ROASTED WINTER VEGETABLES

 6 lg carrots, peeled
 1 lg parsnip, peeled
 1 lg sweet potato
 1 sm butternut squash, peeled and seeded
 3 tbsp olive oil
 1 ½ tsp salt
 ½ tsp fresh black pepper
 2 tbsp fresh parsley, chopped

Cut vegetables into 1 inch cubes, place in single layer on baking sheet.

Drizzle with olive oil and sprinkle with salt and pepper. Toss well and bake in 425°F oven for 35-minutes, until all vegetables are tender.

Sprinkle with parsley and serve hot.

CARROT CAKE

Non-stick cooking spray (to grease baking dish)
<u>Batter</u>
1 ½ c sugar
4 lg eggs, beaten
¾ c oil
2 c rice flour (or flour blend of choice)
2 tsp xanthan gum
2 ½ tsp baking soda
1 tsp cider vinegar
2 tsp baking powder
Pinch salt
1 tsp all spice
2 tsp cinnamon
1 can crushed pineapple (11 oz)
2 c carrots, finely grated
1 c raisins
<u>Cream Cheese Frosting</u>
1 8-oz pkg creamed cheese
1 tsp butter
1 c icing sugar
1 tbsp vanilla extract

~

Preheat oven to 350°F, coat 9" bunting pan with cooking spray.

Grate carrots and drain pineapple; set aside

Put eggs in large mixing bowl and mix well. Add in sugar and oil and mix well. Mix in GF flour, xanthan gum, ½ tsp baking soda, baking powder, salt, all spice and cinnamon. Batter should be thick.

Dollop the remaining soda in the middle of the batter and add the cider vinegar directly on top to create a fizzle reaction, then blend well and completely.

Add remaining ingredients and mix until well blended.

Bake 1 hour in 350°F oven until knife inserted comes out clean.

For the frosting, beat the creamed cheese and butter with the sugar and vanilla until smooth. Spread the frosting over the top of the cake.

4.

Family Day

Eggplant Lasagne came from two sources, one, my dad had this dying eggplant that needed some TLC and once it started to produce, it really produced and I had to use these lovely vegetables. And two, I wanted an alternative to the heaviness of the gluten-free pasta so we didn't come away from the meal feeling so bloated. Previously, I had never cooked with eggplant and what a pleasure it is to discover a new way to create a favourite dish.

You can find an easier desert than cottage pudding. Great to assemble when time is of the essence, but you want something tasty to end the meal.

~ Menu ~

Baked Stuffed Mushrooms

Caesar Salad

Eggplant Lasagne

Garlic Toast

Cottage Pudding

BAKED STUFFED MUSHROOMS

24 2" fresh mushrooms
2 tbsp butter
⅓ c GF bread crumbs
⅛ tsp pepper
Sprigs parsley
1 tbsp olive oil
3 tbsp finely chopped green onion
2 tbsp chopped parsley
2 oz feta cheese, crumbled

~

Preheat oven to 450°F

Remove stems from mushrooms and peel outside (dirt) off mushrooms. Finely chop enough of the stems of mushrooms to measure ¾ c, set aside. Place the mushroom caps and oil in a large bowl, toss to coat evenly. Arrange the mushroom caps, stem less side up on a cookie sheet and set aside.

In medium saucepan melt butter over moderate heat, add green onion and sauté until soft, about 2 minutes. Add chopped mushroom stems and sauté until tender, about 2 more minutes. Stir in GF bread crumbs, parsley and pepper until well mixed. Remove saucepan from heat, stir in cheese and mix well.

Spoon mixture into each cap to fill; bake in oven until heated through and lightly browned, about 10-minutes. Transfer mushrooms to serving platter and garnish with fresh parsley to serve.

CAESAR SALAD

    Romaine lettuce hearts, washed, trimmed
    1 lemon
    1 c parmesan cheese, grated
    ½ c bacon bits
    <u>Dressing</u>
    1 egg yolk
    2 tbsp GF Worcestershire sauce
    1 tbsp Dijon mustard
    2 tbsp minced garlic
    1 tsp anchovy paste
    1 ½ c olive oil
    ½ c parmesan cheese, grated
    1 tsp sugar
    OR <u>Vinaigrette</u>
    2 cloves garlic, minced
    ¼ c oil
    2 tbsp lemon juice
    Salt to taste
    ¼ tsp pepper
    ¼ tsp dry mustard
    ¼ tsp sugar
    5 tbsp parmesan cheese
    ~

Shred romaine hearts in large bowl, cut lemon in half and squeeze juice, remove seeds, over the lettuce and mix. Add in parmesan and bacon bits, toss to mix, top with dressing.

<u>*Dressing*</u>

Combine egg yolk, GF Worcestershire sauce, Dijon, garlic and anchovy paste in bowl. Whisk in oil to thicken, then add parmesan cheese. Refrigerate for two hours until chilled.

To serve, shake or whisk until well blended and smooth and add salt and pepper to taste.

<u>*Vinaigrette*</u>

Combine all ingredients in jar with tight-fitting lid and shake well. Makes about ½ c.

EGG PLANT LASAGNE

Non-stick cooking spray
3 lg eggplants
1 ½ lbs lean burger
1 bay leaf
1 lg can tomatoes
1 tsp garlic, minced
2 pieces sun dried tomatoes in oil
1 tsp salt
1 tsp oregano
½ tsp thyme
1 tbsp sugar
Dash pepper
1 can tomato paste
Sliced roma tomatoes

<u>Filling</u>
1 lg container cottage cheese
2 tbsp parsley
½ tsp pepper
2 eggs
1 tsp salt
2 c mozzarella cheese
¼ c parmesan cheese
~

Slice eggplant thinly, place on cookie sheet and bake on each side for 5 minutes.

In large pot, fry garlic and sun dried tomatoes together in a tsp of the oil from the sun dried tomatoes. Add in burger cook until meat is cooked through. Add in tomatoes, tomato paste, spices and sugar and blend well. Top with bay leaf and simmer for two hours.

For the filling, in large bowl, mix cottage cheese with eggs, parsley, pepper and salt and blend well.

Spray bottom of large casserole dish with non-stick cooking spray and line with layer of eggplant. Dash parmesan cheese over eggplant and then layer on the meat mixture. Sprinkle with mozzarella cheese before placing another layer of eggplant and sprinkling with parmesan cheese. Top this layer with the cheese filling and mozzarella. Top with another layer of eggplant, sprinkle first with parmesan and then mozzarella and top with thinly sliced tomatoes. Dash with pepper to taste.

Bake in 350°F over for 1 hour. This has a tendency to be a bit watery, so halfway through the cooking time, pull the lasagne out of oven and drain excess fluid with large soup ladle. Return to oven to finish cooking time. Once done, let stand 5-to-10-minutes to set before serving.

GARLIC TOAST

Ends of Udi bread
½ c butter
2 cloves garlic, minced
2 tbsp parsley, chopped or dried
~

Blend butter, garlic and parsley until smooth, spread on bread and toast under broiler in oven.

COTTAGE PUDDING

<u>Basic Cake</u>
½ c butter
1 c white sugar
2 eggs
1 tsp vanilla
1 ½ c rice flour
1 ½ tsp xanthan gum
½ tsp baking soda
½ tsp cider vinegar
3 ½ tsp baking powder
½ tsp salt
1 c milk
<u>Sauce</u>
1 c brown sugar
1 ½ c water, boiled
1 tsp vanilla
2 tbsp corn starch
1 tsp butter
~

Cream butter and sugar together until well mixed, add eggs and beat until creamy. Gradually add in milk and remaining liquid ingredients. Add 1 c of the flour, xanthan gum, salt and baking powder, mix well. Add the soda in middle of batter and then the cider vinegar on top to create the sizzle, mix in well with batter and add remaining flour and dry ingredients. Blend well.

Bake in 350°F oven for 35-40-minutes until knife inserted comes out clean.

For the sauce, boil 1 c water in medium saucepan. Blend corn starch and sugar together in bowl and mix with ½ room temperature water and then pour into boil water to blend well and thicken. Remove from heat, add vanilla and butter and serve over cake.

5.

Hockey Night

Now, this meal is just plain fun and super easy!

The caramel popcorn is now something my kids request for those 'bring to school' special treat days around Christmas and the end of the school year. Okay, I'll admit it, even hubby likes to have some to bring to the office to share.

~ Menu ~

Prosciutto wrapped peppers with Feta

Corn Bread

Texas Chilli

Caramel Popcorn & Chocolate

PROSCIUTTO WRAPPED PEPPERS WITH FETA

4 peppers various colours
½ brick feta cheese
2 pkg prosciutto meat
~

Empty peppers of seeds and slice thickly, (each pepper makes about 6-slices), line with slice of feta cheese and wrap in prosciutto.

Line on cookie sheet and bake for 20-minutes at 350°F. Serve hot.

CORN BREAD

¾ c cornmeal
1 ¼ c milk
1 c GF flour
1 tsp xanthan gum
½ tsp soda
½ tsp cider vinegar
⅓ c sugar
1 tbsp baking powder
½ tsp salt
1 egg
¼ c oil
~

In large bowl mix corn meal and milk together in bowl and set aside for 5-minutes.

Preheat oven to 350°F

Add GF flour, sugar, baking powder, salt, egg and oil to mixture, stir until blended. Add soda in middle of mixture and place cider vinegar on top to create fizz. Mix well until blended.

Fold out to loaf pan and cook for 20-minutes, until knife inserted in middle comes out clean.

Can also be made in muffin pan for individual serving with chilli.

TEXAS CHILI

1 tbsp oil
1 c chopped onion
2 cloves garlic

1 lb hamburger
1 lg can tomatoes
¾ tsp cumin
¼ tsp salt
⅛ tsp pepper
⅛ tsp cayenne pepper
2 can kidney beans (2x9oz)
1 can kernel corn nibblets (9oz)
1 can chopped green chillies (4.5oz)
1 container fresh ricotta (or cottage) cheese
1 egg
2 c shredded Monterey Jack cheese
1 pkg 5" GF soft corn tortillas wraps
~

Preheat oven to 325°F

Sautee onion and garlic in bottom of large cooking pot with oil for one minute until clear. Add hamburger and fry together until cooked on medium heat.

Add tomatoes, spices, beans and corn and simmer for two hours.

Mix together ricotta cheese, green chillies, 1 c of Monterey Jack cheese and egg and blend. Separate mixture between the five GF wraps and roll up.

Layer a small amount of chilli along the bottom of a 9" casserole dish, place five rolled GF wraps along the top and then layer remaining chilli and top with remainder of Monterey Jack cheese.

Bake in preheated oven for 1 hour.

CARAMEL POPCORN & CHOCOLATE

1 c un-popped kernels / 24 c popped corn
1 c butter, cut in chunks
2 c firmly packed brown sugar
½ c light corn syrup
2 tbsp molasses
½ tsp salt
¾ tsp soda
1 ½ tsp vanilla
2 Aero chocolate bars, melted

~

Place popped corn in large roasting pan.

Preheat oven to 250°F. Line a cookie sheet with parchment paper.

In medium saucepan over low heat, melt butter. Add brown sugar, molasses, corn syrup, stirring gently until mixture begins to boil, continue until the soft ball candy stage 240°F.

Remove pan from heat and add in salt, baking soda and vanilla. Pour over the popcorn in long streams, folding the popped corn until completely covered.

Place the roasting pan in oven and bake for 15-minutes. Using a spatula, lift, flip and coat the popcorn and continue to bake another 20-mintes. Cool for 5-minutes and transfer to baking sheet and let cool an additional 15-minutes before drizzling with melted chocolate.

Break into serving sized pieces and serve.

Can be stored in airtight container for up to a week.

6.

Groundhog Day

This meal I owe to my oldest boy who wanted breakfast for supper.

It reminded me of when we were kids and indeed use to have breakfast for supper over Lent. Knowing that perhaps some would prefer a more vegetarian meal, I have included the extras for good measure.

~ Menu ~

Hot Artichoke Dip

Sour Cream Pancakes

Spinach with Strawberries

Lasagne Wraps

Rice Pudding

HOT ARTICHOKE DIP

  1 green onion, chopped
  1 can artichoke hearts, drained
  ¼ tsp paprika
  2 tbsp parmesan cheese, grated
  1 clove garlic, minced
  ½ c mayonnaise
  ¼ c cream cheese
  Black pepper
  2 tbsp green onions, thinly sliced (for garnish)

~

Preheat oven to 350°F.

Combine green onion and garlic in chopper and process until well minced together.

Add paprika, parmesan, garlic, mayonnaise, cream cheese and pepper and blend until smooth.

Transfer to small baking dish and bake for 20-minutes until bubbly.

Serve hot and garnish with green onion.

Goes well with chips or vegetables.

SOUR CREAM PANCAKES

2 eggs, separated
¼ c sugar
1 c sour cream
2 tbsp butter, melted
1 c GF flour (minus 2 tbsp)
2 tsp xanthan gum
1 tsp soda
1 tsp cider vinegar
½ tsp salt
1 tsp baking powder

~

Beat egg whites until they form peaks. Add sugar and beat 2 minutes; set aside.

Using the same beater; beat yolks until light in color. Stir in sour cream and melted butter.

Mix GF flour, xanthan gum, salt and baking powder together; add to sour cream mixture and combine well. Fold in beaten egg whites, top with soda and pour cider on top of soda to create fizz, mix well.

Cook in hot oiled skillet turning to brown each side. You will know when it is time to turn the pancake when small air bubbles form on surface.

SPINACH WITH STRAWBERRIES

Fresh spinach, torn
2 c strawberries, cut in half
½ c almonds (not coated)

<u>Dressing</u>
¼ c sugar
1 ½ tsp chopped onion, minced
¼ tsp GF Worcestershire sauce
¼ tsp paprika
½ c oil
¼ c cider vinegar

~

In salad bowl, toss spinach, strawberries and almonds together.

Mix all dressing ingredients together and pour over salad to coat

LASAGNE WRAPS

8 uncooked GF lasagne noodles
10 oz pkg frozen chopped spinach, thawed with all moisture squeezed out
1 c parmesan cheese, grated
1 ⅓ c cottage cheese
½ tsp salt
½ tsp pepper
2 cloves garlic, minced
1 lg onion, chopped
2 tbsp oil
14 oz can tomato sauce
1 tsp sugar
½ tsp basil
½ tsp oregano leaves

~

Cook GF noodles according to package directions.

Preheat oven to 350°F

Mix spinach, ¾ c parmesan, cottage cheese, salt and dash of pepper together in mixing bowl. Spread mixture along the length of lasagne noodle, roll noodle and stand on end in greased 7-8" casserole dish

Saute garlic and onion in oil until onion is clear, 2 minutes. Add tomatoe sauce, sugar, salt and remaining spices and simmer uncovered for 5-minutes. Pour over noodles and cook for 30-minutes. Remove from oven and sprinkle with remaining parmesan cheese.

RICE PUDDING

    1 c short grain white rice
    5 c water
    1 slice lemon peel
    1 tbsp butter
    Pinch salt
    2 c hot milk (preferably whole)
    2 c sugar
    5 egg yolks
    Cinnamon to garnish

~

In medium saucepan, bring water to boil with lemon peel, butter and pinch of salt.

Add in rice and let simmer for about 20-minutes.

Stir occasionally.

When most of the water has evaporated, add in very hot milk, simmer for five minutes and add sugar.

In separate bowl, beat together egg yolks and add a few spoonfuls of rice mixture to temperate the egg yolks. Then add the now warm egg mixture to the saucepan and stir quickly until even.

Serve in large dish and sprinkle with cinnamon.

7.

Zorba the Greek

Although the Donair is not traditional Donair meat, it is easy to prepare though timely to cook. The sauce makes lots, so feel free to cut the ingredients in half. The sauce can be frozen though for future use on pizzas or subs.

~ Menu ~

Hummus

Greek Salad

Donairs

Souvlakia

Tzatziki

Greek Honey Puffs

HUMMUS

1 can garbanzo beans, drained and rinsed
1 tbsp lemon juice
½ tsp salt
3 tbsp sesame tahini paste
¼ c olive oil
Dash pepper
3 cloves garlic, minced
¼ c red pepper, minced

~

Combine all ingredients in food processor until blended and smooth. Serve with fresh vegetables.

GREEK SALAD

1 head romaine lettuce, trimmed and torn into bite sized pieces
1 c black olives
½ container feta cheese, crumbled
1 cucumber, English, chopped in chunks
12 cherry tomatoes, halved
1 sm red onion, sliced
1 sm green pepper, seeded and cut in chunks
1 sm red pepper, seeded and cut in chunks
2 stalks celery, chopped

<u>Dressing</u>
¼ c oil
½ c red wine vinegar
3 tbsp honey
½ tsp salt
Dash dry mustard
1 tsp mint, crushed
Dash oregano, thyme and anise seed, crushed

~

In large salad bowl, toss all ingredients together to combine.

<u>*Dressing*</u>

In bowl, whisk all ingredients together until smooth.

Pour over salad and toss to coat.

DONAIR

3 lbs burger
2 tsp garlic, minced
2 tsp onion, minced
2 tsp red (cayenne) pepper
2 tsp paprika
2 tsp white pepper
1 tsp sugar
1 tsp salt

~

In large bowl, mix all ingredients together and knead well.

Place in foil-lined pan with cookie sheet underneath and cook in 350°F oven for 1-1/2 hours. Cover the last 45-minutes with foil.

<u>Sauce</u>
1 can carnation milk, whipped
1 ½ c sugar
Dash dried garlic powder to taste
Mix all together and slowly add up to ¼ c vinegar to mixture.

~

Spoon meat mixture onto GF wraps and top with sauce, add lettuce and diced tomatoes, wrap and serve.

SOUVLAKIA

1 ½ lb boneless lamb shoulder
¼ c dry red wine
¼ c lemon juice
¼ c olive oil
2 cloves garlic, minced
1 tbsp dried oregano
1 tbsp dried rosemary
2 tsp grated lemon rind
1 bay leaf
¼ tsp pepper
½ in
~

Trim excess fat from lamb, cut lamb into 4 by ½" strips and set aside. In shallow dish, whisk together remaining ingredients and add lamb to marinade, turning to coat thoroughly. Cover and refrigerate for 4 hours, up to 24-hours, stirring occasionally.

Just before serving, remove lamb from marinade, reserving marinade, thread lamb accordion-style onto skewers, place on barbeque and grill over medium high heat for 6-to-8-minutes, turning often and basting with marinade until tender but still pink on the inside.

TZATZIKI

    2 c plain yogurt
    1 lg cucumber
    1 tsp salt
    3-5 cloves garlic, minced
    2 tbsp fresh dill, finely chopped
    1 tsp white wine vinegar
    ¼ tsp pepper
    2 tbsp olive oil

~

Line sieve with cheese cloth, set over bowl and spoon yogurt into sieve, cover and let drain in fridge for 2 hours.

Peel, seed and coarsely grate cucumber, place in colander, sprinkle with salt, cover with a plate small enough to fit inside colander, let drain 1 hour. Rince cucumber and pat dry on paper towel.

In medium bowl, combine yogurt, cucumber, garlic, dill, vinegar and pepper. Stir in olive oil, a little at a time until well blended.

GREEK HONEY PUFFS

3 c GF flour
3 tsp xanthan gum
2 tsp soda
2 tsp cider vinegar
1 tbsp plain yogurt
1 pkg yeast
½ c lukewarm water
½ tsp baking powder
1 tsp sugar
½ tsp salt
1 ½ lukewarm water
2 c oil
Ground cinnamon (for serving)

<u>Syrup</u>
2 c sugar
1 stick cinnamon
1 c water
½ c honey

~

Dissolve yeast in ½ lukewarm water and set aside

In medium bowl, mix 2 ½ c GF flour, xanthan gum, baking powder, sugar and salt, mixing to combine.

Add dissolved yeast, yogurt and 1 ½ lukewarm water to dry ingredients and mix well with mixer for about 3 minutes on medium speed, making sure there are no lumps. Add soda and then the cider vinegar to create the fizz, blend well, adding remaining flour. Cover bowl with plastic wrap and set aside in warm place for two hours until batter has doubled in size.

For the syrup, add sugar, cinnamon stick, water and honey to saucepan and boil for five minutes until the sugar is completely dissolved, keep warm.

When batter is doubled in size, heat 2 cups of oil in saucepan or deep frying pan until very hot, but not smoking. Using two spoons, drop by the teaspoon the batter for each puff into the hot oil. Turn the puffs using a slotted spoon and fry until golden brown on each side. Remove to plate lined with paper towel to absorb excess oil.

Dip the hot puffs in syrup and then sprinkle with cinnamon and more sugar if desired.

Serve warm.

8.

Mardi Gras

Anything Disney related is a hit in our world. This came after a visit to Disneyland where they were so accommodating with their Gluten-Free abilities. I though if they can do it, so can I and here is the result of a bit of a trip through the bayou, Disneyland style.

~ *Menu* ~

Tossed Salad with Honey Mustard Dressing

Crab Soup

Barbequed Shrimp

Catfish Casserole

Chocolate Truffle Cheesecake Brownies

TOSSED SALAD WITH HONEY MUSTARD DRESSING

Fresh lettuce greens, torn
Tomatoes, diced
Cucumber, chopped
1 c mayonnaise
1 tbsp honey
1 tbsp Dijon mustard
2 tsp lemon juice
1 tbsp sugar
Salt and pepper to taste

~

Toss lettuce greens, tomatoes and cucumber in salad bowl.

Combine all dressing ingredients together and whisk for 3-5 minutes until well blended.

Place in fridge until ready to use.

CRAB SOUP

    2 c heavy cream
    1 sm container of half and half
    1 c milk
    1 c potatoes, finely diced
    1 c carrots, finely diced
    ½ lb crabmeat
    ½ c frozen corn kernels
    ½ tsp salt
    ¼ tsp pepper
    ¼ c water
    1 tbsp cornstarch
    1 c clam juice
    2 tbsp green onion, chopped
    1 tbsp dill

~

Heat heavy cream, half and half and milk to a simmer, add potatoes, carrots, crabmeat, corn, salt and pepper; reducing heat, simmer, stirring occasionally to cook vegetables through, about 15-minutes.

Mix cornstarch and water in small dish until smooth, add to soup, bring to a boil to thicken.

Serve garnished with green onions and dill.

BARBEQUE SHRIMP

    1 lb med shrimp
    1 tbsp Cajun spice
    1 tsp coarsely cracked peppercorns
    2 tbsp olive oil
    ½ c onion, chopped fine

2 cloves garlic, minced
2 c water
2 tbsp lemon juice
1 tbsp GF Worcestershire sauce
¼ c dry white wine
1 tsp salt
1 bay leaf
2 c heavy cream
2 tbsp butter, room temperature
~

Peel and devein the shrimp, leaving tails on and reserving the shells for the sauce.

Mix together 1 tbsp of Cajun spice with ½ tsp cracked black pepper, run mixture into shrimp. Store shrimp, covered until ready to use.

Heat 1 tbsp of olive oil over medium high heat in saucepan, add onion and garlic and cook for 1 minute. Add the shells, water, lemon, GF Worcestershire sauce, dry white wine, and remaining Cajun spice and cracked peppercorns and bay leaf. Bring mixture to a boil, reduce heat and simmer for 15-minutes.

Remove pan from heat and allow mixture to cool, then strain into small saucepan, disregard solids and bring to a boil and cook for another 15-minutes until liquid is reduced to ¼ cup, thick, syrupy and brown.

Heat remaining 1 tbsp of olive oil in saucepan and add shrimp and cook stirring for 2 minutes, add cream and sauce and simmer for 3-5-minutes.

CATFISH

<u>Tomato Compote</u>
2 med tomatoes
1 tsp butter
2 green onions, chopped
1 clove garlic, crushed
1 tbsp tomato paste
1 tbsp basil
Salt and pepper to taste

<u>Cheese Rice</u>
½ c water
½ c half and half
2 tsp salt
1 c instant rice
1 c pepper jack cheese
4 tbsp butter

<u>Catfish</u>
4 catfish fillets
3 tbsp butter
4 tbsp Cajun spice
3 tbsp oil

~

<u>*Tomato Compote*</u>

Cook tomatoes in oven on low temperature for 1 hour.

Add butter to saucepan and saute green onion and garlic and medium pan for 3-5-minutes until tender. Once tomato is cooled, peel and remove seeds and chop fine. Combine with tomato paste and add to sautéed garlic and green onion. Add basil, salt and pepper to taste. Simmer on low for 1 hour.

Rice

Bring water and half and half to a boil. Add rice and cook until done. Add cheese, butter and salt and pepper and stir until melted and blended. Rice should be creamy. If mixture is too stiff, add more milk.

Catfish

Pat catfish dry, brush with melted butter and generously season each side with Cajun spice, coating well. Heat oil in skillet over medium-high heat, add fish and fry for 3-4 minutes on each side, until cooked through.

For serving, add rice in centre of each plate, top with catfish and garnish with dollop of tomato compote.

CHOCOLATE TRUFFLE CHEESECAKE BROWNIES

<u>Brownie</u>
12 squares semi-sweet chocolate, chopped
¼ c butter
2 eggs
½ tsp salt
½ c sugar
1 tsp vanilla
⅔ c GF flour
1 tsp xanthan gum
½ tsp soda
½ tsp cider vinegar

<u>Topping</u>
1 pkg cream cheese, softened
½ c sugar
2 tbsp butter
2 tbsp milk
3 squares semi-sweet chocolate, melted
2 eggs
1 tbsp corn starch

~

Preheat oven to 350°F.

Heat chocolate and butter over medium heat in saucepan until chocolate is melted. Stir in sugar and blend well.

Using a hand mixer, on low, beat in eggs and vanilla. Stir in salt and GF flour and xanthan gum, mix well. Add soda in a heap in the middle of the batter and pour the cider vinegar on top to create the fizz, mix well.

Spread mixture onto well greased 9" square baking dish.

Topping

In a large mixing bowl, beat together cream cheese, sugar and butter until creamy.

Beat in eggs, milk, corn starch and stir in melted chocolate. Pour over brownie base and bake for 40-minutes.

Cool completely and drizzle with melted chocolate.

9.

St. Patrick's Day

Stew was an absolutely staple growing up in my house. If it was in the fridge, it was going in the stew. Easy, filling and great the next day.

~ Menu ~

Dill Dip

Irish Stew

Boston Cream Pie

DILL DIP

    1 c mayonnaise
    1 c sour cream
    1 tsp parsley flakes
    1 tsp dill weed, dried
    ½ tsp onion powder
    ½ tsp celery salt
    ~

Mix all ingredients together.

Chill until needed and service with chips or vegetables.

IRISH STEW

2 lb boneless beef chuck roast
3 tbsp oil
1 c onion, chopped coarsely
2 c new potatoes, chopped
2 c carrots, chopped
2 c turnip
½ tsp salt
½ tsp pepper
½ tsp paprika
½ tsp garlic, minced
4 c water
1 cube GF beef bouillon

~

Cut meat into 1" pieces. Put oil in large stew pot and add beef, season with salt and pepper, add in paprika and garlic and cook until just about done, should be a slight line of pink in middle.

Remove from heat and place in bowl for later.

Add water, heat to bring to a boil, stirring often to mix drippings left from cooking the beef. Add vegetables to boiled water and simmer until tender, about 30-minutes.

Add in GF bouillon cube stirring until dissolved.

Take two cooked potatoes and one carrot out of the pot place in deep bowl. Add in some broth puree until smooth. Add back into boiling water to thicken.

Add in beef, reduce heat to low and simmer for 1 hour.

BOSTON CREAM PIE

<u>Basic Cake</u>
½ c butter
1 c white sugar
2 eggs
1 tsp vanilla
1 ½ c rice flour
1 ½ tsp xanthan gum
½ tsp baking soda
½ tsp cider vinegar
3 ½ tsp baking powder
½ tsp salt
1 c milk

<u>Filling</u>
1 c milk
2 tbsp corn starch
¼ c sugar
1 egg
½ tsp vanilla

<u>Glaze</u>
1 c icing sugar
2 tbsp cocoa
1 tbsp butter
4 tsp milk

~

Cream butter and sugar together until well mixed, add eggs and beat until creamy. Gradually add in milk and remaining liquid ingredients. Add GF flour, xanthan gum, salt and baking powder, mix well. Add the soda in middle of batter and then the cider vinegar on top to create the sizzle, mix in well with batter; add remaining dry ingredients. Blend well.

Bake in 350°F oven for 35-40-minutes until knife inserted comes out clean.

Using thread, cut cake into two layers

Filling

Heat milk in heavy saucepan over medium heat to bring to a boil.

Mix cornstarch and sugar in a boil and blend well. Add in egg and vanilla, mix and pour into milk, stirring to boil and thicken. Cool well

Glaze

Beat all ingredients together adding more liquid if necessary to make a barely pourable glaze.

To assemble, spread custard between cake layers. Spread glaze over top. Chill at least one hour before serving. Serve with whipping cream.

10.

The Sinking of the Titanic

The fun I had assembling this meal. The idea came after a visit to the Titanic display marking 100-years since the great ship sank. I did a Google search and everything I found talked about the decadence of being on board, from the cabins, to the cutlery, not to mention the food.

Finding a few menu samples and filling in some gaps, I tried to assemble the full seven course meal for an over-the-top social occasion. If you're going all out on this one, don't forget the nautical theme when placing the table!

~ Menu ~

Baked Onions, Frenched

Grilled Tomato Tummies

Honey-Mint Fruit Salad

Goat Cheese Stuffed Mushrooms

Chicken Lyonnaise

Roasted Pork Loin with Dijon and Rosemary

Roasted Mangoes and Star Anise

Baked Mini Potato Galettes

Asparagus with Oka

Decadent Truffles

BAKED ONION WITH VINAIGRETTE

4 med onions, unpeeled
Coarse salt
1 egg yolk
½ clove garlic, minced
1 tsp wine vinegar
Pinch salt & pepper
½ c grape seed oil
Tarragon, fresh, to taste
Thyme, fresh, to taste

~

Heat oven to 425°F. Cut barely a sliver off the bottom of each onion so they can sit without rolling on a baking sheet. Pierce the skin in a few places to release steam. Make four mounds of salt on the baking sheets and set each onion into mound, so they sit without moving. Bake 15-minutes, then lower temperature to 325°F and continue baking for another 90-minutes.

Vinaigrette

Whisk together egg yolk, garlic and vinegar and season to taste. Beat in the oil in small amounts to keep dressing thick. Add lemon juice as desired. Refrigerate until ready to serve.

Set onions on serving plate (no salt) and slit open to reveal soft inside. Spoon sauce into each onion until it starts to bubble up and out onto the plate. Serve hot.

GRILLED TOMATOES TUMMIES

    4 med tomatoes, unpeeled cut across the belly
    2 tbsp butter
    ½ c cream
    Salt & Pepper to taste

~

In large skillet, melt butter over medium heat and place tomatoes, belly side down without moving to cook for 10-minutes. Make small slits in skin to release steam. Cook on opposite side for another 10-minutes.

Towards the end of the cooking time, add cream to caramelize.

Serve hot, seasoned with salt and pepper.

HONEY-MINT FRUIT SALAD

    2 honeycrisp apples, corded and cubed
    1 mango, peeled and cubed
    1 c blueberries
    1 c strawberries, quartered
    1 lime, juiced
    1 tbsp honey
    6 mint leaves, fresh, thinly sliced
    1 tbsp unsweetened coconut

~

In large bowl, combine apples, mango and berries.

In small microwavable dish, mix lime juice and honey and microwave on high for 20-seconds to soften honey. Pour over fruit.

Add mint and gently toss to combine.

Sprinkle with coconut just before serving.

GOAT CHEESE-STUFFED MUSHROOM

¼ c white wine
1 tbsp olive oil
1 tbsp fresh thyme
1 tsp garlic paste
Pinch salt
¼ tsp pepper
1 lb mushrooms, stems removed
1 c Goat cheese
1 tsp fresh chives, chopped, divided

~

Preheat oven to 375°F.

In a bowl, toss together wine, thyme, garlic paste, salt, pepper and mushrooms. Marinade for 5-minutes.

In separate bowl, mix goat cheese and 1 tsp chives.

Remove mushrooms from marinade and stuff with goat cheese mixture until just rounded on the top.

Place on baking sheet and bake for 20-minutes and then broil for 2-3-minutes until cheese is slightly golden.

Garnish with remaining chives.

CHICKEN LYONNAISE

⅓ c GF flour
⅓ tsp xanthan gum
1 tbsp Thyme
½ tsp salt
½ tsp pepper
6 boneless chicken breasts
1 egg, beaten
3 tbsp oil
2 onions, sliced thin
1 clove garlic, minced
⅓ c white wine
1 c GF chicken stock
2 tsp tomato paste
Pinch sugar

~

In plastic freezer bag, shake together GF flour, xanthan gum, 1 ½ tsp Thyme, salt and pepper together.

One at a time, dip chicken in egg and toss chicken breasts in bag to coat.

In large skillet, heat 2 tsp of oil over medium high heat. Place chicken in pan, skin side down. Cook turning once, for 10-minutes until golden brown. Remove from skillet and place in 225°F oven.

Reduce heat to medium; add remaining oil to skillet; stir in onions, garlic, and remaining Thyme. Cook, stirring often for 5-minutes or until onions are clear. Increase heat to medium high and continue to cook onions for five minutes more until golden brown.

Add wine to pan; cook stirring to scrape up any brown bits for about 1 minute or until reduced to half. Stir in GF stock, tomato paste and sugar. Boil for 2 minutes or until thickened, Return chicken to pan, turning to coat and cook for 5 minutes or until juice from teh chicken run clear.

ROASTED PORK LOIN WITH DIJON AND ROSEMARY

1 pork loin roast, bone in
1 tbsp Dijon mustard
½ tsp salt
1 tsp pepper
2 springs fresh rosemary

~

Preheat oven to 375°F. Slice pork alongside rib bones to open loin meat away from bone, like a book.

Spread mustard inside cut, season with salt and half the pepper and tuck in rosemary. Sprinkle remaining seasoning over surface of the roast.

Tie meat and bones together with butcher twine, place meat, bone side down on a wire rack set inside a rimmed baking sheet. Roast on middle rack for 90-minutes. Reduce heat to 325°F and roast another 60-minutes until meat is thermometer registers 160°F when inserted into the thickest part of the roast.

Rest 20-minutes, remove twine and bones, slice and serve with Roasted Mangoes and Star Anise

ROASTED MANGOES AND STAR ANISE

2 mangoes, peeled and cut into wedges
1 tbsp ginger
1 tbsp sugar
4 tsp lime zest, divided
2 tbsp lime juice, divided
4 whole star anise, lightly crushed into large pieces
1.2 tsp olive oil
Dash salt
1 tbsp butter

~

Preheat oven to 400°F.

Place mangoes, ginger, sugar, 2 tsp lime zest, 1 tsp lime juice and star anise in bowl; toss to combine.

Heat oil in oven safe skillet over medium heat. Add mango mixture and salt, stirring to coat with oil and place on middle rack of oven. Bake for 7-10-minutes until mango wedges are lightly browned.

Gently toss with butter and remaining lime zest and juice just before serving.

BAKED MINI POTATO GALETTES

3 tbsp olive oil
½ c shallots, chopped fine
2 lbs Yukon Gold potatoes (4 large), peeled and sliced thin
1 tbsp Thyme
½ tsp salt
½ tsp pepper
1 c cheddar cheese
½ c parmesan cheese

~

This dish can be prepared in muffin tray or baking dish; if using baking dish, increase baking time by 10-minutes.

Preheat oven to 400°F.

Line muffin tin with squares of foil, coated with cooking spray. Foil should extend over muffin cup edges to create handles. Set aside.

In small skillet add oil and shallots, cooking over medium heat until tender but not browned, about 2-minutes. Remove from heat and cool completely.

In bowl, combine potatoes with shallots, thyme, salt and pepper until well coated. In another bowl, combine cheddar and parmesan cheese.

Place a layer of potato in bottom of each muffin tin, sprinkle with a heaping teaspoon of cheese mixture into each cup. Repeat layers gently pressing potatoes to pack down until all ingredients are used and muffin tins are full; finish each with cheese mixture on top.

Bake on middle rack in oven until tops are golden and potatoes are tender when pierced with fork, about 40-minutes.

Let rest 10-minutes before lifting out of tin and serving.

ASPARAGUS WITH OKA

1 c GF vegetable broth
1 tbsp cornstarch
1 tbsp tarragon leaves
2 tsp Dijon mustard
2 tbsp butter
1 ½ lbs asparagus, fresh, ends trimmed
¼ c red pepper, chopped
1 c Oka cheese, shredded

~

Combine broth, cornstarch, tarragon and mustard in small bowl; set aside.

Melt butter in large skillet at medium heat until butter starts to turn brown; add in asparagus and stir often for three minutes.

Stir broth mixture into skillet; heat to boil; reduce heat and simmer for 3 minutes. Remove from heat and stir in red pepper.

Transfer to serving dish and sprinkle with cheese.

DECADENT TRUFFLES

4 bars of favourite GF chocolate bars
1 ½ c heavy cream
¼ tsp salt
¼ tsp cinnamon
Bottle of cherries, no stems, drained (optional)
¼ c cocoa powder

~

Heat cream until steaming, but not boiling.

In a large bowl, break chocolate bars into chunks and pieces; pour cream over bars and stir until chocolate melts and mixture becomes and a rich "chocolate" brown.

Add in salt and cinnamon; stir to blend.

Leave mixture to cool until slightly hardened, but still soft.

Boil some water and place in small cup with 2 spoons.

On small plate, pour out cocoa powder.

Dip spoon into chocolate to turn out a rounded wedge of chocolate. Place cherry in middle and use other spoon to mould chocolate around cherry. Roll in cocoa and place on serving platter.

Serve chilled

11.

Easter Lunch

I personally love French Onion Soup and had to have a Gluten-free option.

After the heaviness of the French Onion Soup, the lightness of the desert is sure to please.

~ Menu ~

Fruit Salad with Pineapple Dressing

Honey Berry Bread Pudding

Spinach and Sweet Onion Quiche

French Onion Soup

GF Graham Wafer Cheese Desert

FRUIT SALAD WITH PINEAPPLE DRESSING

3 oranges, peeled, sectioned
2 apples, peeled and chopped
2 bananas, sliced
½ green grapes, halved
½ red grapes, halved
1 c coconut (optional)

<u>Dressing</u>
14 oz can crushed pineapple, drained
1 c sour cream
2 tbsp honey
2 tbsp orange rind

~

Place fruit in large salad bowl and toss.

Mix all dressing ingredients together and pour over fruit to coat.

Serve cold.

HONEY BERRY BREAD PUDDING

8 c GF bread cubed
2 c frozen mixed berries
6 eggs
1 ½ c 18% cream
¼ c honey
1 tsp vanilla
½ tsp cinnamon
Warm honey

~

Spread cubes in buttered 13x9" glass baking dish. Sprinkle berries over bread.

In large measuring bowl, whisk eggs until frothy. Whisk in cream, honey, vanilla and cinnamon; pour evenly over bread mixture.

Cover with plastic wrap and refrigerate overnight.

Let pudding stand at room temperature while preheating oven to 350°F.

Bake uncovered for 30-40-minutes or until golden brown; puffed and when a knife inserted in middle comes out clean.

If top browns too quickly, cover loosely with foil.

Serve drizzled with more honey.

GF PIE SHELL

    1 ½ c GF flour
    1 ½ tsp xanthan gum
    ½ c cornstarch
    1 tbsp sugar
    ½ tsp salt
    1 tbsp ice water
    1 lg egg, lightly beaten egg
    ¾ c butter

~

Measure dry ingredients into a large mixing bowl. Use a large whisk to thoroughly blend ingredients.

Pour the dry ingredients into a food processor bowl, fitted with a metal blade.

Add the cold butter cubes and pulse until the butter cubes are reduced to the size of peas and the mixture looks like coarse, dry crumbs.

Add the lightly beaten egg and pulse just until egg is incorporated into the flour-butter mix.

Add 1 tbsp of ice water and pulse several times. Remove the processor lid and squeeze a small amount of the dough in your hand. If it holds together don't add more water. If the dough is too crumbly and dry, add 1/4 teaspoon additional ice water and pulse several more times. Check the consistency of the dough again. If the dough holds together and you can form a ball don't add more water. Adding too much water will make the dough sticky and harder to roll out and shape.

Scrape the dough, which will look crumbly, on a clean, gluten free work surface covered with waxed paper. Gather the crumbly dough into a ball. Flatten to a large disk shape. Wrap in waxed paper and refrigerate for at least one hour before rolling out the dough. At this stage, the dough can be frozen. Place wax paper wrapped dough in a freezer bag, label and freeze for future use.

To Roll Dough: Remove dough from refrigerator and place dough between two sheets of waxed paper. Let dough sit just until its soft enough to roll. When workable, roll lightly from the center outward, working to make a circle about 10-inches in diameter and about 1/8" thick. If the dough should get too warm and sticky, place it in the freezer for several minutes and then continue rolling it.

Peel top sheet of wax paper from the dough and carefully flip the dough, on the remaining sheet of waxed paper, over pie plate. Gently peel the waxed paper from the dough.

Gently press the dough into the pie plate.

Trim edges with knife and crimp edge with a fork or using your favorite method.

SPINACH AND SWEET ONION QUICHE

9" deep-dish GF pie shell, unbaked
1 tbsp butter
1 c sweet onion, chopped, about ½ large
½ tsp salt, divided
8 oz frozen chopped spinach, thawed, drained
4 eggs, beaten
1 c 18% cream
1 c milk
Pinch nutmeg
Pinch pepper
½ c Swiss cheese, shredded

~

Preheat oven to 375°F.

In large skillet, melt butter over medium heat; sauté onion and ¼ tsp salt for 2 minutes. Reduce heat to medium low and sauté another 8 minutes or until golden brown. Transfer to bowl and let cool.

In large bowl, whisk eggs until blended; whisk in cream, nutmeg, remaining salt and pepper. Stir in onion, spinach and Swiss cheese. Pour mixture into pie shell.

Bake about 55-minutes or until edges are puffed and knife inserted into middle comes out clean.

Let stand 10-minutes before serving.

EGGS IN A BASKET

2 tbsp olive oil
2 onions, sliced
2 cloves garlic, minced
1 red pepper, cut lengthwise
1 green pepper, cut lengthwise
2 tomatoes, seeded and quartered
Salt & Pepper
4 eggs
8 slices prosciutto ham

~

Heat oil in pan and cook onions until soft.

Add in garlic and peppers and cook until tender before adding in tomatoes and seasoning with salt and pepper to cover and cook for 10-minutes.

Remove lid and continue to cook until juices have evaporated and everything is soft.

In separate pan cook ham slightly until curled.

Crack eggs into onion/pepper/tomato mixture, spacing them evenly apart, cover and cook until just done.

Take the ham and place on plates (4) and add egg with onions, peppers and tomatoes as the base onto top of ham as though settling into a nest.

Serve hot.

FRENCH ONION SOUP

4 c onion, sliced wafer thin
¼ c butter
8 c boiling water
6 GF beef bouillon cubes
1 tsp salt
¼ tsp pepper
1 clove garlic, minced
Mozzarella cheese
Parmesan cheese

~

Blanch sliced onions by covering in boiling water covered for 5 minutes.

Drain well.

Melt butter in frying pan, add drained onions and sauté until limp. Do not brown.

In large pot mix the water with the bouillon cubes and stir until dissolved.

Add sautéed, butter onions and spices. Cook for 15 minutes.

Spoon soup in dishes, cover with cheese and bake under broiler to melt cheese.

GF GRAHAM WAFER CHEESE DESERT

1 ½ c GF graham wafer crumbs
½ c brown sugar
¼ c butter, melted
<u>Filling</u>:
1 container cream cheese
1 c icing sugar
1 pkg dream whip
Strawberries to garnish

~

Mix GF graham wafers, brown sugar and butter until blended. Reserve ½ c of mixture for topping. Press remainder into bottom of 8x8" baking dish.

<u>Filling:</u>
Beat cream cheese with blender until smooth.

Add in icing sugar and the dream whip. Pour mixture on top of crumbs and sprinkle with remaining ½ c of GF graham cracker crumbs and cover with strawberries

12.

May Day

A simplistic meal for any day of the week! The key here is how to thicken the sauces without loosing the flavour.

For any of the baking, the trick is to know when to add the soda and cider vinegar. Sounds too awful to think that these can be added without taking away from the flavour, but it's true! When I first started 'experimenting' with my recipes, I was so frustrated at the texture (taste aside) until a young clerk at one of the Gluten-free shops told me to try adding in both a 'moist-maker' and the soda and cider to promote 'air' within the batter. I have never looked back.

One note of caution though, everything in moderation. Sometimes you can inadvertently add too much soda and that nice, light-looking, fluffy cake comes out of the oven and practically falls to the floor as it collapses in on itself.

~ Menu ~

Mixed Greens with Buttermilk Coconut Dressing

Beef Stroganoff

Fettuccini

Basic Cake

Frosting

MIXED GREENS WITH BUTTERMILK COCONUT DRESSING

Lettuce greens, torn
Tomatoes, diced
Celery, chopped
Cucumber, chopped

<u>Dressing</u>
⅓ c buttermilk
¼ c sour cream
¼ c mayonnaise
¼ c coconut milk
2 tbsp oil
2 tbsp red wine vinegar
1 tsp sugar
Salt and pepper

~

In salad bowl toss together lettuce greens, tomatoes, celery and cucumber.

<u>Dressing</u>

Process in food processor if possible and blend until smooth. Serve cold.

BEEF STROGANOFF

- 1 ½ tbsp butter
- 1 lb beef fillet cut postage stamp size
- 2 tsp butter
- 1 c onion, chopped
- 2 c mushrooms, sliced
- 2 tbsp cornstarch
- ¼ c water
- 2 GF beef bouillon cubes
- 1 ¼ c boiling water
- ⅛ tsp pepper
- ¼ tsp paprika
- ⅔ c sour cream

~

Heat first amount of butter in saucepan, add beef and sauté until browned well. Transfer meat to small bowl for later use.

Add second amount of butter to saucepan, add onion and mushrooms and sauté until soft.

Mix cornstarch and cold water together until smooth.

Dissolve GF bouillon in boiling water and stir into onion mixture. Add in cornstarch mixture and stir until smooth and thickened. Reduce heat to a simmer.

Add pepper and paprika, stir and then the meat and sour cream. Mix to blend thoroughly.

FETTUCCINI

1 pkg GF Fettuccini noodles
2 tbsp butter
1 ½ c frozen peas
1 red pepper, slivered
2 tbsp cornstarch
¼ c water, cold
¼ c parmesan cheese
½ c milk
¼ c creamed cheese

~

Cook noodles according to package directions, drain and return to pot.

Heat butter in frying pan, add peas and red pepper and sauté until tender, about 4 minutes.

Mix cornstarch and water together until smooth, add to frying plan and stir until smooth and thickened. Stir in milk and creamed cheese and continue to stir until mixed thorough, thickened and smooth.

Pour over fettuccini, mix well and sprinkle with parmesan cheese to serve.

BASIC CAKE

½ c butter
1 ½ c GF flour
1 ½ tsp xanthan gum
1 tsp soda
1 tsp cider vinegar
1 tbsp cream cheese
1 c sugar
2 eggs
1 tsp vanilla
3 ½ tsp baking powder
½ tsp salt
1 c milk
~

Preheat oven to 350°F

Cream sugar and butter together until smooth, add eggs and beat until creamy. Add milk, blend well and then add, GF flour, xanthan gum, baking powder, salt and vanilla, blend well. Add soda to mixture, top with cider vinegar to fizz and mix well with other ingredients. Add cream cheese and blend until smooth.

Bake for 35-40 minutes until knife inserted comes out clean.

BASIC FROSTING

1 c icing sugar
2 tbsp butter
4 tsp maple syrup
~

Blend until smooth and spread on cake

13.

Cinco de Mayo

Another, just for fun of it meal idea. Due to being corn based for their bread, tacos, etc., most Mexican food is already Gluten-free, it just comes down to the knowing and double checking the ingredient list.

The Five-layer dip, along with the Taco Salad are items that I will typically bring along with me when attending a pot-luck, super easy and always a crowd pleaser.

~ Menu ~

Fresh Salsa

Guacamole

Five layer dip

Taco Salad

Salsa chicken

Mexican Taco Steak

Spicy Rice

Strawberries and Chocolate

FRESH SALSA

    3 plum tomatoes, halved and seeded
    1 sm red onion, peeled and quartered
    1 jalapeno pepper, seeded
    1 tbsp cilantro leaves, washed and dried
    2 tbsp fresh lime juice
    Dash pepper
    1 clove garlic, minced
    ½ yellow pepper, seeded and cut in strips
    1 tsp oregano leaves, washed and dried
    ½ tsp salt
    ½ red pepper, seeded and cut in strips
    ~

Combine all ingredients in a chopped and process until combined and chunky.

Serve with corn chips.

GUACAMOLE

    2 avocadoes, ripe, pitted
    1 plum tomato, seeded and cut into small pieces
    2 tbsp fresh lime juice
    2 tbsp cilantro leaves, washed and dried
    Black pepper
    1 sm red onion, peeled and quartered
    2 cloves garlic, minced
    ½ jalapeno pepper, seeded and sliced
    ½ tsp salt
    ~

Combine all ingredients in chopped and process until smooth.

Serve with fresh vegetables

5 LAYER DIP

1 sm container creamed cheese
1 sm container sour cream
2 c salsa
1 lb hamburger
1 pkg GF taco seasoning
2 c cheddar cheese
½ c chopped green onions
½ c chopped tomatoes
½ c shredded, chopped lettuce

~

Cook hamburger and GF taco seasoning according to directions. Drain of grease and cool.

Blend together creamed cheese and sour cream and spread evenly over the bottom of a large casserole (9") dish, layer with hamburger, spread evenly, ensuring that the layers do not mix, then top with salsa in the same manner. Sprinkle to coat top with cheddar cheese and top with lettuce, then green onions and tomatoes.

Serve cold with corn tortilla chips

TACO SALAD

2 c shredded lettuce
1 c cheddar cheese, grated
½ c tomatoes, diced
1 c corn tortillas, crushed
½ c GF salsa
¼ c sour cream

~

Put all ingredients, except crushed tortillas in bowl and mix well.

Serve with crushed tortillas over the top.

SALSA CHICKEN

    4 large chicken breasts
    2 c corn tortillas, crushed
    1 c cheddar cheese, grated
    Salsa
    Sour Cream

~

Rinse chicken breasts in water, lightly pat on paper towel.

Put crushed tortillas in large freezer bag, add in chicken breast one at a time and shake to coat. Lay coated chicken breast in greased casserole dish, sprinkle with cheddar cheese and top with a line of salsa.

Cook in 350°F oven for 45-minutes, until done.

Serve with a dollop of sour cream.

MEXICAN TACO STEAK

    2 lbs sirloin steak
    1 pkg GF taco seasoning mix
    2 tbsp brown sugar
    1 ½ c tomato juice

~

Place steak in dish large enough to hold, or a sealable plastic bag. Combine all ingredients and pour over steak to marinade and put in fridge for 4-to-24-hours.

Remove steak from marinade, drain excess, and grill until done.

SPICY RICE

    2 c uncooked rice
    1 c GF salsa
    1 c water
    ~

Add water and salsa together in saucepan, heat to boil. Add rice and cook until done.

STRAWBERRIES AND CHOCOLATE

    4 Aero bars
    2 c strawberries
    ¼ c whipping cream
    Dash nutmeg
    Vanilla ice cream
    ~

Melt Aero bars over low heat in saucepan, add whipping cream and nutmeg to blend well.

Cut strawberries, rinse and allow to dry in colander. Mix with melted chocolate just before serving.

Put scoop of ice cream in each bowl and cover with strawberry mixture.

14.

Mother's Day

If they are going to have a day for us moms, why not make it a decadent meal of favourites.

~ Menu ~

Baked Tomatoes

Asparagus Ham Rolls

Cream of Cold Carrot Soup

Beef Bourguignon

Chocolate Dainties

BAKED TOMATOES

3 tbsp butter
⅔ c onion, chopped fine
½ tsp salt
Dash pepper
1 tsp parsley
½ tsp basil
5 med tomatoes

~

Melt butter in saucepan, add onion, salt, pepper, parsley and basil and sauté until onion is soft.

Overlap tomatoes in bottom of 9x13" casserole dish. Spoon mixture evenly over top being sure to get some on each tomato.

Bake in 350°F until hot and bubbly, about 20-25-minutes.

ASPARAGUS HAM ROLLS

12 GF Udi bread slices
Butter
12 cooked ham slices
12 asparagus spears, canned or freshly cooked
12 deli cheese slices

~

Roll bread slices lightly with rolling pin until thin.

Spread with butter.

Add slice of ham, cheese and place an asparagus on one side. Roll and secure with toothpick.

Baste with butter.

Place on baking sheet and brown in 400°F oven for 10-minutes.

CREAM OF COLD CARROT SOUP

    2 med onions
    3 tbsp butter
    1 tsp curry powder
    ½ tsp dill seed
    2 lbs (12) carrots
    5 c chicken stock
    Salt & Pepper to taste
    Pinch of nutmeg
    1 ½ - 2 c heavy cream
    Fresh parsley

~

Chop onions into coarse chunks. Sweat onions in saucepan or stock pot until clear.

Stir in curry powder and dill seed and continue to cook for 2 minutes.

Slice carrots (reserving 1 for garnish).

Combine carrots and onion mixture and add chicken stock. Season with salt, pepper and nutmeg. Cook for 30-minutes.

Puree the mixture in a separate bowl in 3-4 batches. Chill thoroughly.

Just before serving, stir in cream, adjust seasoning and garnish each bowl with a carrot curl and a spring of parsley or dill.

If served hot, add cream gradually to pureed carrot mixture and heat gently, without bowling

BEEF BOURGUIGNON

- 3 tbsp olive oil
- 2 lbs beef tops, cut 1" thick
- 1 c mushrooms, quartered
- 1 tbsp cornstarch
- 2 tbsp water
- 3 tbsp tomato paste
- 1 ½ c Burgundy wine
- 1 tbsp coarse salt
- 1 tsp black pepper, fresh
- 2 bay leaves
- 1 c GF beef broth
- 4 tbsp butter, softened

~

Heat olive oil in sauce pan and sear beef tips in medium high heat on all sides, cooking 5-8-minutes.

Add onions, mushroom and tomato paste.

Mix cornstarch with water until smooth and add to mixture. Stir well to thicken, 5-6-minutes then add wine, stirring to loosen browned bits from bottom of pan.

Add salt, pepper, bat leaves, and GF beef broth. Cover and reduce heat to low, simmer for 45-minutes, stirring occasionally.

Remove from heat, stir in butter and serve.

CHOCOLATE DAINTIES

<u>Cream Cheese Filling</u>
1 container cream cheese
⅓ c + 1 tbsp sugar
1 egg
1 tsp vanilla

<u>Streusel topping</u>
½ c sugar
4 tbsp GF flour
¼ tsp xanthan gum
¼ tsp soda
¼ tsp cider vinegar
1 ½ tsp cinnamon
4 tbsp butter, softened

<u>Chocolate Cake</u>
1 c firmly packed brown sugar
¼ c vegetable oil
3 eggs
3 oz semisweet chocolate, melted and cooled
½ c buttermilk
½ c blue berries
1 tsp vanilla
2 c rice flour (or flour blend of choice)
2 tsp xanthan gum
1 tsp soda
1 tsp cider vinegar
1 tsp baking powder
2 tbsp vegetable oil (to grease baking dish

~

<u>Cream Cheese Filling</u>

Mix cream cheese, sugar, egg and vanilla in mixer on low speed until well combined; set aside.

Streusel Topping

Mix sugar, GF flour, xanthan gum, and cinnamon together with a fork. Add soda and then the cider vinegar to create the fizz and mix well. Add in butter to mixture until crumbly, resembling peas; set aside.

Cake

Preheat oven to 350°F, coat 9" baking dish with cooking spray

In large bowl, mix together eggs and brown sugar with oil and beat until creamy. Add in chocolate, blueberries, buttermilk and vanilla and blend.

Add in baking powder, xanthan gum and GF flour, mix well until blended.

Dollop the soda in the middle of the batter and add the cider vinegar directly on top to create a fizzle reaction; blend well.

Pour batter in pan and bake until a toothpick inserted comes out clean, approximately 35-40-minutes. Let cake stand for 5-minutes in pan before turning out onto a cooling rack to cool completely.

Assembly

Preheat oven to 375°F. Spray muffin pans with cooking spray to coat, or line with baking cups.

Fill each muffin cup halfway with chocolate cake batter. Spoon about a tablespoon of cream cheese mixture on top. Sprinkle with streusel topping over muffins.

Bake for 18-20 minutes, until knife inserted comes out clean. Note that cream cheese filling should remain moist. Cool 10-minutes before removing from moulds.

15.

Fun Friday

~ Menu ~

BAKED TACOS

CHOCOLATE PUDDING

BAKED TACOS

    1 pkg GF soft shells
    1 lbs burger
    1 pkg GF taco seasoning
    1 c water
    1 c cheddar cheese, shredded
    1 c sour cream
    1 c GF salsa

~

In large skillet, fry burger. Add water and taco seasoning; bring mixture to a boil and simmer until reduced. Transfer meat to paper towels to drain off excess grease.

Spray a large casserole dish with cooking spray.

To assemble, take a GF wrap, place a line of taco meat off center, but not too close to the edge; top with a thin line of salsa and cheddar cheese. Roll and place in a single layer in casserole dish.

Once all wraps are rolled and in casserole dish, top with more salsa and cheddar cheese; place in 350°F oven for 35-40-minutes, until bubbly.

To serve, top with a dollop of sour cream

CHOCOLATE PUDDING

1 ½ c milk
3 tbsp cornstarch
3 tbsp cocoa
½ c milk
1 tsp vanilla
⅓ c sugar

~

Heat first mount of milk until boils, be sure not to burn.

Mix cornstarch, cocoa and second amount of milk until smooth.

Stir into boiling milk until returns to boil and thickens.

Remove from heat, add vanilla and sugar, stir until smooth.

PARTY MIX

2 c GF Honey Nut Chex® cereal
2 c GF Cinnamon Chex® cereal
2 c GF Honey Nut rings
2 c GF Cinnamon rings
1 c GF pretzels
¼ c butter
¼ c brown sugar, packed
2 tbsp honey
1 tsp cinnamon
½ tsp nutmeg
¼ tsp ground cloves
2 c mini marshmallows

~

In large microwavable bowl, place cereals. In 2 c microwavable measuring cup, add butter, honey and brown sugar. Microwave on high for 2 minutes, stirring after 1 minute, until mixture is bubbly.

Stir in spices.

Pour over cereal and stir until coated.

Microwave mixture uncovered for 3 minutes, stirring and scraping bowl after every minute.

Cool slightly, about 5 minutes before adding in marshmallows. Spread on waxed paper.

Store in airtight container.

16.

Father's Day

Meat-o-saursus best describes the males in my house, so when it came to dad's day, that was top of mind. Favourite desert, the always easy apple crisp, topped with vanilla ice-cream.

~ Menu ~

Pork Skewers with Dipping Sauce

Corn and Red Pepper Chowder

Barbequed Beef

Spicy Fries with dip

Apple Crisp

PORK SKEWERS WITH DIPPING SAUCE

18 skewers
6 boneless loin centre chops cut into 3 strips each
1 tsp garlic paste
1 tsp ginger paste
1 tsp ground cumin
1 tsp salt
2 tsp olive oil, divided
⅓ c GF apricot jam (most are GF, but check)
⅓ c Dijon mustard
1 tsp fresh rosemary

~

Preheat oven to broil and place rack in centre.

Place wooden skewers in water and set aside.

Place pork strips in bowl and coat with garlic and ginger pastes, cumin, salt and ½ tsp olive oil. Marinade for 10-minutes.

Insert skewers through the length of each pork strip, place on a rimmed baking sheet and drizzle with remaining oil. Broil for 5-7 minutes until cooked through and lightly golden.

While pork skewers are cooking, in separate bowl, stir together jam, mustard and rosemary.

Serve with warm pork skewers.

CORN AND RED PEPPER CHOWDER

1 tbsp butter
2 stalks celery, chopped fine
2 cloves garlic, minced
1 onion, chopped fine
1 lg sweet red pepper, diced
Dash salt & pepper
2 c GF chicken broth
4 red potatoes, cut in ½" cubes
3 c corn kernels
2 tbsp corn starch
1 ½ c cream
2 c water
Basil, fresh, chopped

~

In large pot, melt butter over medium heat; sauté celery, garlic, onion, red pepper, salt and pepper for about 5 minutes, until onions are softened.

Stir in broth, potatoes, corn, 2 c water and bring to boil over high heat. Reduce heat, cover and simmer for 10-minutes until potatoes are almost tender.

Increase heat to medium; whisk cornstarch into cream and gradually stir into pot. Simmer, uncovered for 5 minutes, stirring often, until slightly thickened (do not let boil). Season to taste with salt and pepper.

Ladle into bowls and sprinkle with basil.

If prefer thicker chowder, add more cornstarch to milk mixture.

BARBEQUE BEEF

    1 tbsp oil (for cooking)
    1 lb sirloin beef, thinly sliced
    5 scallions
    1 tbsp sugar
    1 tbsp sesame oil
    2 tbsp GF soy sauce
    1 tsp garlic paste
    1 tsp ginger paste
    ~

In a medium bowl, mix ginger and garlic, with GF soy sauce, and sesame oil.

Slice beef into thin strips. Cut off the white of the scallions and slice vertically into thin strips to match beef. Chop across middle to make medium pieces. Add beef to scallions and mix. Pour sauce over beef to coat, cover and let stand to marinate for three hours.

Heat oil in large, deep pan and pour in marinated beef and marinade and fry until meat turns a rich golden brown.

SPICY FRIES

<u>Dip</u>
½ c mayonnaise
1 tsp garlic, minced
¼ tsp lemon juice
½ tsp Dijon mustard
Pinch paprika
1 tsp GF Worcestershire sauce
½ tsp Cajun spice
Salt and pepper to taste

<u>Fries</u>
1 tbsp garlic, minced
½ tsp Cajun spice
⅓ c parmesan cheese, grated
1 tsp parsley
½ tsp salt
1 bag frozen plain shoe string fries

~

<u>Dip</u>

Mix together all ingredients in blender and set in fridge until ready to use.

<u>Fries</u>

Mix together all ingredients except fries and pour in to large bowl for use when fries are cooked. Cook fries according to oven directions. While hot transfer to large bowl to coat with mixture.

Serve hot with dip.

APPLE CRISP

6 c apples, peeled, cored and sliced
½ c brown sugar, packed
1 tbsp lemon juice
½ tsp cinnamon

Topping

½ c GF flour
½ tsp xanthan gum
1 c GF Oats (as an alternate, un-sweetened coconut is good as well)
⅓ c butter
½ c brown sugar
½ tsp cinnamon

~

Preheat oven to 350°F.

Combine apples, lemon juice, sugar and cinnamon together and transfer into a 8" baking dish.

Mix all ingredients together for the topping and spread evening over apples. Spread to fill crevices.

Bake for 55-minutes, top with ice-cream.

17.

Taste of the Maritimes

A taste of home really. Having grown up on the ocean, simply smelling the dishes in preparation will take me back in time.

When I was growing up, my cousin and I were always sent 'up the hill' to pick the berries during the season. I use to think they called this desert Blueberry Grunt because of all the bending over!! Apparently 'grunt' dates back to the colonial days and the sounds emitted from the pot while the desert was cooking.

~ Menu ~

Cranberry Bread

Salmon Salad

Clam Chowder

Caramelized Scallops

Scallop Casserole

Blueberry Grunt

CRANBERRY BREAD

    2 c GF flour
    2 tsp xanthan gum
    1 ½ tsp soda
    1 tsp cider vinegar
    ¾ c sugar
    1 ½ tsp baking powder
    1 tsp salt
    1 tsp orange rind
    1 c cranberries, halved
    2 tbsp oil
    1 egg, beaten
    ¾ c orange juice
    ~

Preheat oven to 350°F. Grease 9x5" loaf pan.

Sift together GF flour, xanthan gum, sugar, baking powder, ½ tsp soda, salt, orange rind and cranberries. Combine egg, oil and orange juice. Add to dry ingredients and mix until just blended. Add remaining soda to top of mixture and pour cider vinegar over the top to create the fizz, mix well until all blended.

Place in loaf pan and cook for 50-minutes until knife inserted comes out clean.

SALMON SALAD

1 c salmon, cooked and flaked
1 c celery, diced
1 c carrots, diced and cooked
1 c peas, cooked
1 tbsp onion, minced
2 c GF macaroni pasta, cooked
2 tbsp lemon juice
½ tsp sugar
Butter lettuce

<u>Blender Mayonnaise</u>
1 egg
1 tsp Dijon mustard
1 ½ tsp vinegar
¼ tsp salt
1 c oil
2 tbsp lemon juice
1 tbsp boiling water

~

In large bowl, mix together salmon, celery, carrots, peas, onion and GF macaroni.

Combine lemon juice, sugar, blender mayonnaise until well mixed and smooth. Pour over vegetable, macaroni and salmon mixture and toss until well combined. Serve over crisp lettuce leaves.

Blender Mayonnaise

Place egg, mustard, vinegar, salt and ¼ c of oil in container and blend until frothy. Add remainder of oil in slow steady steam while blending until mixture thickens. Add lemon juice to taste and then water. Blend until thick and smooth.

CLAM CHOWDER

    4 tbsp butter
    2 c chopped onion (2 onions)
    2 c medium diced celery (4 stalks)
    2 medium chopped carrots (6 carrots)
    4 c diced potatoes (8 potatoes)
    ½ tsp thyme
    1 tsp salt
    ½ tsp pepper
    4 c clam juice
    4 tbsp corn starch
    ½ c water (cold)
    2 c milk
    3 c chopped clams

~

Melt butter in large pot, add onions and cook over medium heat for 10-minutes or until clear. Add celery, carrots, potatoes, thyme, salt and pepper and sauté for 10 more minutes. Add clam juice and bring to a boil, simmer, uncovered for 20 more minutes until vegetables are tender.

Mix cornstarch and cold water until well blended and smooth, add to vegetables and stir to thicken. Add in milk and clams and heat through to cook clams.

Season to taste with salt and pepper.

CARAMELIZED SEA SCALLOPS

2 c salt
2 c hot water
8 c cold water
12 lg sea scallops (about 1 ¾ lb)
2 tbsp butter
½ lemon (optional)

~

Line baking sheet with paper towel. Combine the 2 c of salt with the hot water in a large bowl, stirring to dissolve salt. Add the cold water. Add the scallops to the brine and let stand for 10-minutes (no longer as the scallops will become too salty). Drain the scallops, rinse under cold water and arrange in a single layer on paper towels.

Heat the butter in saucepan over medium high heat until it ripples and begins to smoke. Sprinkle scallops lightly with salt and add them to the butter without crowding. Cook without moving the scallops until the bottoms are a rich golden brown, 3 to 3 ½ minutes. Turn the scallops and do the same to the other side.

Transfer scallops to serving platter and serve with a squeeze of lemon juice on top.

SCALLOP CASSEROLE

1 c rice, cooked
1 lb scallops, uncooked
Salt & Pepper to taste
1 lg onion, chopped
1 green pepper, diced
1 c mushrooms, sliced
1 c frozen peas
½ c GF bread crumbs
4 tbsp butter

Sauce
2 tbsp corn starch
1 ¼ c milk
¼ tsp salt
Pinch pepper
Pinch nutmeg
½ c cheddar cheese, grated
~
Preheat oven to 375°F

In saucepan, using 2 tbsp of butter, sauté onions until clear, about 2-minutes, add in green pepper and mushrooms, cooking an additional 5 minutes until tender.

For the sauce, heat 1c milk in microwave for 2 minutes and then put in saucepan to continue the heating process, stirring to ensure the milk does not burn. In small glass mix ½ c milk with cornstarch until blended and smooth. Add to heated milk, ensuring no lumps and whisk until thickened. Add in salt, pepper, nutmeg, stir until mixed; removing sauce pan from heat, add in cheese until blended and melted.

Place the cooked rice at the bottom of a casserole dish, then layer the onion, green pepper and mushroom mixture evenly on top. Top this with the frozen peas. Season with salt and pepper to taste.

Place scallops over vegetables and cover with cheese sauce. Melt butter and pour over GF breadcrumbs to mix together, sprinkle over cheese layer.

Bake in over for 20 minutes until bubbly. Do not overcook as scallops will become dry and tough.

BLUEBERRY GRUNT

1 qt blueberries
½ c water
½ c sugar
1 ½ c GF flour
1 ½ tsp xanthan gum
1 tsp soda
1 tsp cider vinegar
2 tsp baking powder
¼ tsp salt
1 tsp sugar
1 tbsp butter
⅔ c milk

~

Heat blueberries, water and first amount of sugar together in saucepan until blueberries begin to soften; then bring to a boil, simmering gently for 5-minutes while making dumplings

Sift together GF flour, xanthan gum, baking powder, salt and sugar. Cut in butter and add enough milt to make a soft dough. In middle of mixture, add soda and then the cider on top of the soda to create the fizz. Mix until just blended.

Drop the dumpling dough, by the spoonful onto the hot blueberries (makes approximately 10). Cover tightly (no peaking) and cook for 15-minutes without raising the lid.

Serve hot with ice cream.

18.

Grading Day

At the end of the school year when summer is laid out in front of them, kids want to celebrate. You can almost taste the sunshine in the Ice Cream Sodas! But there has to be some nutrition in there somewhere, doesn't there? Depends on how you dress it, they may never know that they had something healthy for their celebration of another year accomplished.

~ Menu ~

Ice Cream Soda

Pizza Mix Appetizers

Cranberry Chops

Dressed Mashed Potatoes

Green Bean Casserole

Marshmallow Chocolate Squares

ICE CREAM SODA

    1 container fresh strawberries, hulled and sliced
    ½ c sugar
    1 lemon, juiced
    3 tbsp syrup (as combined above)
    1 tbsp vanilla
    3 tbsp cream
    Club soda
    Vanilla ice cream

~

Strawberry Syrup

Combine strawberries, lemon juice and sugar in container, cover and refrigerate overnight. Strain the syrup into a pitcher, pushing on berries to extract all liquid.

Assembly

Pour syrup, vanilla, and cream in tall glass; mix with fork. While whisking, add club soda until glass is ¾ full. Add 2 scoops ice cream, then soda to fill glass. Serve with a spoon and straw.

PIZZA MIX APPETIZERS

1 lb bacon, cooked and cut
1 ½ c green pepper, chopped
1 egg
1 ½ c diced cheddar cheese
1 bottle chilli sauce
GF Udi Bread

~

Heat oven to 450°F.

Mix all ingredients, except GF Udi Bread together and spread on squares of Udi Bread.

Bake on cookie sheet for 5-7-minutes. Turn oven off and leave squares in 5 more minutes until bubbly and bread is toasted underneath.

CRANBERRY CHOPS

1 ½ tsp sage, divided
1 tsp garlic, minced
1 tsp thyme
½ tsp allspice
½ tsp paprika
2 apples, peeled, cored and thinly sliced
4 boneless pork chops
⅔ c whole berry cranberry sauce
1 tbsp GF soy sauce

~

Spread half of thinly sliced apples evenly over bottom of greased casserole dish, top with pork chops; set aside.

Mix cranberry sauce with 1 tsp sage, garlic, thyme, allspice, paprika and GF soy sauce and spoon evenly over pork chops.

Top with remaining apple slices and sprinkle with remaining sage.

Bake in 350°F oven 45-50-minutes, until done.

DRESSED MASHED POTATOES

2 ½ lbs Yukon Gold potatoes, peeled and cut into 1" chunks
2 clove garlic, smashed
2 tbsp butter
1 c sour cream, divided
½ c chives, fresh and chopped
½ c bacon bits
1 c cheddar cheese, shredded

~

Add potatoes and smashed garlic to boiling water in large pot and cook until potatoes are tender, about 25-minutes. Strain and return to pot. Add potatoes and ⅔ c sour cream to mash potatoes until smooth and creamy. Stir in ⅔ of the chives and bacon bits.

Spread mixture into casserole dish and bake in 400°F oven for 15-minutes. Sprinkle with cheese and bake an additional 5-minutes until cheese is melted.

Top with remaining sour cream, chives and bacon bits.

GREEN BEAN CASSEROLE

    5 c hot tender-cooked cut green beans
    1 c heavy cream
    1 can mushroom pieces
    1 tbsp corn starch
    ¼ c cream cheese, softened
    1 tbsp GF soy sauce
    Dash pepper
    Dash salt

~

Place beans in shallow baking dish.

In small bowl, combine cream with cornstarch to mix well; add in cream cheese, GF soy sauce, salt and pepper. Add in mushroom pieces last and pour over beans, stirring to coat.

Bake in 350°F oven for 30 minutes. Let stand 5 minutes before serving.

MARSHMALLOW CHOCOLATE SQUARES

    ¼ c butter
    4 tbsp cocoa
    1 can sweet milk
    2 ½ c GF graham wafer crumbs
    1 package mini marshmallows

~

Melt butter and cocoa in large pot.

Add in can of sweet milk and mix thoroughly. Remove from heat and add in GF graham wafer crumbs to mix thoroughly. Add in mini marshmallows and spread in 9"x9" casserole dish.

Chill and serve.

19.

Canada Day

Could be Canada Day, the Forth of July, a family reunion, or whatever is special to celebrate, the summer is a great time to do it and this simple meal will be a bit without the sweat.

Most of this is a make-ahead preparation so the day and the festivities that accompany the meal can be enjoyed to the fullest.

~ Menu ~

Lemonade

Picnic Salad

Barbeque Sauce

Steak Medallions

Potato Salad

Corn on the Cob

Onions in the Skin

Summer Breeze

LEMONADE

    12 lemons
    10 c sugar
    7 c water, boiled
    ~

Squeeze juice from lemons, put in saucepan and heat over medium heat. Add sugar and stir to dissolve.

Chill.

To serve, mix 1 part of lemon syrup with 3 parts cold water.

PICNIC SALAD

5 med red potatoes
2 c fresh green beans, cut into 2" pieces
1 med red pepper, seeded and cut into strips
1 c frozen corn, thawed
1 celery stalk, thinly sliced
1 med carrot, shredded
3 green onions, thinly sliced
1 ½ c mozzarella cheese

<u>Dressing</u>
⅔ c olive oil
2 cloves garlic, minced
¼ c white wine vinegar
2 tbsp thyme, minced
1 tsp salt
½ tsp sugar
½ tsp pepper

~

Cut potatoes into ½" slices, place in large saucepan, cover with water, boil and cook until done, usually 20-minutes.

Place beans in saucepan, cover with water, bring to a boil and cook until tender-crisp, approximately 10-minutes.

Drain both potatoes and beans.

In large salad bowl, combine red pepper, corn, celery, carrots, onions, and cheese. Add in cooled potatoes and beans. Toss to mix.

In small bowl combine all ingredients for vinaigrette and blend well. Pour over vegetables and toss to coat.

Serve chilled.

BARBEQUE SAUCE

    1 c ketchup
    1 c water
    ¼ c vinegar
    1 onion, minced
    1 clove garlic, minced
    ½ tsp salt
    1 tbsp GF Worcestershire sauce
    2 tbsp brown sugar
    2 tbsp molasses
    2 tsp dry mustard
    1 tsp chilli powder (to taste)
    ~

Blend all ingredients together well, put in saucepan, bring to a boil and gently simmer for 25-minutes.

Freezes well.

STEAK MEDALLION

Marinade with sauce 1-2 hours before serving.

Grill using medium high heat, turning only once.

POTATO SALAD

    6 med potatoes, cooked and diced
    1 c celery
    2 tbsp onion, minced
    2 tbsp green onion, chopped
    1 tsp parsley
    4 eggs, hard boiled
    1 tsp salt
    ½ tsp pepper
    1 ½ c mayonnaise
    ⅓ c milk
    1 tsp Dijon mustard
    1 tsp sugar
    Dash paprika

~

In bowl, place cooled, cooked potatoes, add celery, onion, green onion, parsley, eggs, salt and pepper, toss to mix.

In small mixing bowl, combine mayonnaise, milk, Dijon sugar together to blend well.

Pour over potato mixture and toss to coat.

Sprinkle with paprika and serve cold.

CORN ON COB

    Corn cobs in skin
    water

~

Soak corn, in skin in water to cover for 2 hours. Drain. Cook on grill 5-10-minutes to steaming.

Serve hot.

ONIONS IN SKIN

    4 onions in skin

~

Place on barbeque and cook for 20-25-minutes. Squeeze out of skin to serve.

Fresh, soft and sweet.

SUMMER BREEZE

    1 c GF chocolate cookie crumbs
    1 tbsp butter
    1 can frozen concentrated juice, thawed (mixed berry, lime or pink lemonade)
    2 tbsp icing sugar
    1 container cool whip

~

Combine crumbs and butter and press into 9" spring form pan, place in freezer for 15-minutes.

Mix cream cheese, juice and icing sugar in blender and blend on high speed until smooth, pour into large bowl and fold in whipped topping.

Pour mixture over crust and freeze for approximately four hours.

Remove from freezer 10-minutes before serving.

20.

Birthday Celebrations

~ Menu ~

Yogurt Pops

Marshmallow Fruit Kabobs

Pizza Crust

Pizza Sauce

Toppings

Chocolate Cake

YOGURT POPS

    2 c vanilla yogurt
    ¾ orange juice
    ½ c white grape juice
    ~

Mix ingredients together in blender until well combined.

Divide and pour into 8 small cups.

Place on baking sheet and freeze for 1 ½ hours until partially frozen, insert popsicle sticks in middle.

Freeze an additional 3-4 hours until firm.

MARSHMALLOW FRUIT KABOBS

    1 med banana, cut in 8 pieces
    8 pineapple pieces
    8 lg white marshmallows
    4 bamboo skewers
    1 tbsp butter
    ~

Divide and thread banana, pineapple and marshmallows alternately onto bamboo skewers.

Brush all sides with butter and grill for 1 minute on each side.

PIZZA CRUST

3 c GF flour (reserve some flour for kneading)
3 tsp xanthan gum
1 tsp soda
1 tsp cider vinegar
1 pkg active dry yeast (1 tsp)
2 tbsp oil
1 tsp salt
2 tbsp sugar
1 ¼ c water, warm
1 tbsp Italian seasoning

~

Mix GF flour, xanthan gum, sugar and yeast in large bowl. Add oil and water to mixture and stir well, dough should be sticky. Top with soda and then cider vinegar to create fizz and mix well with other ingredients.

Knead dough on GF floured surface until smooth, form into a ball and set aside for 30-minutes to raise.

Spread dough on pizza pie plate, add sauce and toppings.

PIZZA SAUCE

1 sm can tomato sauce
2 tbsp tomato paste
1 tsp sugar
Italian spices (oregano, sage, thyme)

~

Put all ingredients into small sauce pan and cook for 10-minutes to bring to a boil and set aside.

VEGETARIAN

½ artichoke hearts, cut in quarters
½ c mushrooms, sliced
¼ c red onion, sliced, thin
10 black olives, pitted, sliced
Dash oregano
1 c mozzarella cheese, shredded
½ green pepper, sliced
1 lg tomato, sliced, thin

BACON CHEESEBURGER

½ lb burger
6 slices bacon, cooked crisp and crumbled
¾ c mozzarella cheese, shredded
¾ c cheddar cheese, shredded

BARBEQUE CHICKEN

½ c GF barbeque sauce
2 chicken breasts, skinned, cooked, diced
1 c green pepper, chopped
1 c red pepper, chopped
1 ½ c Colby (or Monterey Jack) cheese, shredded

CHOCOLATE CAKE

Non-stick cooking spray (to grease baking dish)

<u>Batter</u>

1 c firmly packed brown sugar
¼ c vegetable oil
3 eggs
3 oz semisweet chocolate, melted and cooled
½ c buttermilk
¼ c blue berries
1 tsp vanilla
2 c rice flour (or flour blend of choice)
2 tsp xanthan gum
1 tsp soda
1 tsp cider vinegar
1 tsp baking powder
2 tbsp vegetable oil (to grease baking dish

<u>Cream Cheese Frosting</u>

1 8-oz pkg creamed cheese
¾ c confectioners' sugar
½ c cocoa powder
1 tbsp vanilla extract

~

Preheat oven to 350°F, coat 9" baking dish with cooking spray

In large bowl, mix together eggs and brown sugar with oil and beat until creamy. Add in chocolate, blueberries, buttermilk and vanilla and blend.

Add in baking powder, xanthan gum and GF flour, mix well until blended.

Dollop the soda in the middle of the batter and add the cider vinegar directly on top to create a fizzle reaction, then blend well.

Pour batter in pan and bake until a toothpick inserted comes out clean, approximately 35-40-minutes. Let cake stand for 5-minutes in pan before turning out onto a cooling rack to cool completely.

For the frosting, beat the creamed cheese with the sugar, cocoa powder, vanilla until smooth.

Slice the cake in half horizontally (easiest way to do this is using thread wrapped around the cake and saw through cleanly). Spread half the frosting over the top and half between the layers of the cake.

21.

Summer Barbeque

The key to any good picnic is the ability to assemble ahead of time and be able to pack and go.

There is really nothing better than sitting in the outdoors and pulling out a great meal.

~ Menu ~

Lemon Freeze

Grilled Caesar Salad

Ribs

Baked Potato

Sweet and Sour Onions

Strawberry Shortcake

GRILLED CAESAR SALAD

1 GF baguette
8 slices bacon, fully cooked
4 Romaine hearts, cut in half lengthwise
8 slices parmesan cheese
<u>Vinaigrette</u>
2 cloves garlic, minced
¼ c oil
1 tbsp lemon juice
1 tbsp red wine vinegar
Salt to taste
¼ tsp pepper
¼ tsp dry mustard
¼ tsp sugar
5 tbsp parmesan cheese
~

Prepare vinaigrette by combining all ingredients together and mixing well.

Cut bread into 16 slices and lightly brush both sides with vinaigrette.

Grill bread on both sides for 10-seconds each; just long enough to toast and pick up grill marks. Remove from grill and set on a side plate.

Grill bacon for 10-seconds per side and set on plat.

Grill Romaine hearts cut side down for 20-seconds.

To assemble, on each of 8 plates, arrange Romaine lettuce halves, bacon, toast and parmesan cheese. Top with a dollop of vinaigrette and serve.

RIBS

    2 lbs ribs
    ¼ c GF soy sauce
    ½ c brown sugar
    ½ c ketchup
    2 cloves garlic, minced
    ½ tsp cinnamon
    ½ tsp ginger
    ¼ tsp pepper
    ~

Mix all ingredients, except ribs together to blend well.

Pour over ribs to marinade for 2 hours.

Grill ribs, reserving the marinade for basting.

BAKED POTATO

    6 lg baking potatoes
    Sour cream
    Chives
    Bacon bits
    Butter
    ~

Wrap baking potatoes in tin foil, prick with knife throughout and place in oven for 1 hour until soft.

Serve with all the fixin's

SWEET AND SOUR ONIONS

    6 med onions, thickly sliced
    ¼ c cider vinegar
    ¼ c sugar
    1 tsp salt
    ¼ c butter
    ¼ c boiling water
    ~

Lay onions in shallow, greased casserole and sprinkle with salt. Combine vinegar, butter, sugar and water, pour over the onions. Bake uncovered at 350°F for 30 minutes until tender.

For a milder flavour, substitute white vinegar for cider vinegar; for sweeter, use raspberry.

STRAWBERRY SHORTCAKE

    3 c strawberries, crushed
    1 c sugar
    2 c GF flour
    2 tsp xanthan gum
    1 tsp soda
    1 tsp cider vinegar
    4 tsp baking powder
    ⅓ c sugar
    ½ tsp salt
    ½ c butter
    1 c blended (10%) cream or milk
    1 c whipping cream
    ~

Crush cleaned, (top removed) strawberries, sprinkle with sugar to taste(¼ c) and set aside.

Preheat oven to 425°F.

Combine, GF flour, xanthan gum, baking powder, sugar and salt in bowl. Cut in butter and knead until resembles bread crumbs. Add soda on top of mixture, and cider directly on top of soda to create fizz and then blend throughout.

Slowly add light cream or milk to mixture until evenly moistened and mixture clumps together. Knead until just blended (do not over knead, the best biscuits are those just blended) or until ingredients hold together in a ball.

Place dough on GF floured board and roll out to ½" thickness. Using cookie cutter or round plastic cup, cut dough into 2 ½" rounds and arrange on greased baking sheet.

Bake for 10-15-minutes until golden brown. Let cool slightly.

Split shortcake while warm and butter. Placing in individual serving bowl, fill with heaps of crushed berries, top with other half of shortcake, dollop with more berries and whipping cream. Do this for each serving.

22.
Labour Day

Holding tight to the freedom of summertime meals, while moving into the warm comfort food season is the beauty of this meal.

This is the combination of the sweet summer taste of fresh strawberries and the hearty combinations of root vegetables.

~ Menu ~

Stuffed Cherry Tomatoes

Strawberry salad with sweet & garlic dressing

Chicken Cordon Blue Salad

Potato Stack

Carrots and Cranberries

Acorn Squash

Banana Butterscotch

STUFFED CHERRY TOMATOES

16 cherry tomatoes
⅓ c cream cheese
1 tbsp mayonnaise
2 tsp chives, chopped fine
7 bacon slices, cooked crisp, crumbled
~

Remove stems from tomatoes and a small slice from the opposite end. Scoop and discard seeds with spoon leaving hollow shell. Place on paper towel to drain.

Mash cream cheese and mayonnaise together with fork in small bowl until smooth, stir in chives and then add crumbled bacon.

Spoon mixture into small sandwich bag, snip a ½" hole in corner and squeeze 1 ½ to 2 tsp of filling into each tomato shell.

Chill for 3 hours before serving.

STRAWBERRY SALAD WITH SWEET & GARLIC DRESSING

Lettuce
1 lb strawberries, stem removed and cut into chunks
Fresh mint, chopped

<u>Dressing</u>
1 whole garlic bulb
1 tbsp white wine vinegar
1 tbsp extra virgin olive oil
1 tbsp safflower oil
Dab of honey
Fresh cracked black pepper

~

Separate and peel garlic cloves, place in a saucepan with enough water to cover, bring to a boil, reduce heat and simmer until tender, about 15-minutes.

Remove garlic cloves, increase heat and boil liquid until only 2 tbsp remains.

Put cloves in sieve, pour hot liquid over them, mash through into a small bowl using the back of a wooden spoon.

Whisk vinegar and oil into garlic, flavour with honey and pepper

CHICKEN CORDON BLUE CASSEROLE

3 lg chicken breasts, sliced thin
1 pkg deli ham slices
Swizz cheese, grated
Salt & Pepper to taste

~

In 9" square casserole dish, lay out layer of chicken to cover bottom, top with thin layer of swizz cheese, then ham slices, another layer of swizz cheese and top with chicken slices.

Sprinkle remaining swizz on top to cover.

Cook in 350°F for 45-50-minutes.

Casserole tends to get juicy, so siphon off excess juice at about the half hour mark and put back in oven to continue cooking.

POTATO STACK

2 ½ lbs potatoes
1 ¼ c parmesan cheese, grated, divided
1 ¼ c gruyere cheese, grated, divided
2 tbsp olive oil
2 tbsp green onion, chopped fine
2 cloves garlic, minced
1 ½ c heavy cream
Salt and pepper to taste

~

Preheat oven to 350°F. Grease large casserole dish.

Peel and slice potatoes into 1/16" thickness. Do not wash or rinse potatoes. Set aside. Mix the parmesan and gruyere cheeses together and set aside.

Heat oil in saucepan over medium heat, add green onion and cook for about 5-minutes, add garlic and sauté another few minutes until garlic is golden in color; reduce heat to low. Add cream and potatoes and gently stir to coat potatoes and cook until cream starts to thicken; 7-10-minites.

Gently stir in cheese, reserving ⅓ c to coat top of casserole and continue to cook until cheese is melted. Season with salt and pepper.

Transfer potatoes to casserole dish, making sure they are flat and spread evenly in the pan. Sprinkle with reserved cheese.

Cover and bake for 1 ½ hours until potatoes are tender and liquid is absorbed.

CARROTS AND CRANBERRIES

1 ⅓ c orange juice, divided
3 tbsp brown sugar
1 tbsp cornstarch
2 tbsp butter
2 lbs carrots, peeled, sliced thin
1 c cranberries
½ tsp salt
Dash pepper

~

Mix 1 c orange juice and brown sugar together in sauce pan and heat until sugar is dissolved.

Whisk together remaining orange juice with cornstarch until smooth, add to brown sugar mixture, bringing to a boil to thicken; set aside.

Melt butter over medium heat in skillet, add carrots and cook, stirring until tender-crisp, about 5-minutes. Add cranberries, salt and pepper and continue to cook another 2-minutes. Add the thickened orange juice mixture and combine thoroughly; cook about 2-minites until heated through.

ACORN SQUASH

- 2 acorn squash
- ¼ c brown sugar, packed
- ½ c olive oil

~

Preheat oven to 400°F.

Pierce squash with sharp knife and microwave on high for 2-minutes. Cool.

In small bowl mix sugar and oil until well blended.

Cut each squash in half, lengthwise; remove seeds and cut each half into four slices; place in large bowl and toss with marinade to coat. Place cut side down on cookie sheet and bake 45-minutes until tender.

BANANA BUTTERSCOTCH

- 1 c brown sugar
- 3 tbsp butter
- 2 tbsp cream
- ⅛ tsp vanilla
- 3 bananas
- ½ c whipping cream
- 1 tsp sugar
- ½ tsp vanilla

~

Combine sugar, butter, cream and vanilla in saucepan and bring to a boil. Simmer slowly to thicken.

Slice bananas into four dishes

Whip cream, sugar and vanilla until stiff. Spoon hot butterscotch over bananas and top with whipping cream.

23.

Sunday Dinner

The traditional family get together with the traditional family meal flare.

~ Menu ~

Roasted Tomato and Chipotle Chicken Appetizer

Pot Roast

Potato Strata

Ginger Carrots

Braised Pearl Onions with Peas and Bacon

Cherry Cheesecake

ROASTED TOMATO AND CHIPOTLE CHICKEN APPETIZERS

½ c cilantro, divided
1 tsp vegetable oil
¼ c green onion, thinly sliced, white divided from green parts
1 tbsp garlic paste
1 ⅓ c pre-cooked chicken, shredded
1 c chipotle salsa, divided
1 pkg GF wraps
½ c cheddar cheese, shredded
¼ c mozzarella cheese, shredded

~

In a bowl, blend together cheeses.

Preheat oven to 400°F.

Chop half cilantro.

In medium skillet, heat oil and sauté chopped cilantro with white parts of the green onion and garlic paste until onion is softened, about 2-minutes. Stir in shredded chicken and ¾ c salsa and cook on low heat another 2-3-minutes, until warmed through.

Place GF wraps on parchment lined baking sheet, spread with remaining salsa, top with chicken mixture and sprinkle with cheese blend.

Bake for 5-7-minutes until cheese is melted and golden.

Garnish with remaining cilantro and green parts of green onion.

Slice into strips and serve warm.

POT ROAST

Pork Roast
¼ c butter
3 carrots, chopped
4 stalks celery, chopped
½ c onion, chopped
1 clove garlic, minced
1 c mushrooms, chopped
½ c dry red wine
1 c water
1 GF bouillon cube
2 tsp salt
¼ tsp pepper
½ tsp paprika
1 c sour cream
2 tbsp corn starch
~

Smear the butter over the roast and place in large Dutch oven a couple minutes each side.

Add carrots, celery, onion, and garlic to pan and cook a couple minutes until onions are limp. Add in mushrooms. Mix water and bouillon together until blended, add red wine and spices to liquids and pour over roast.

Place a bed of vegetables (potatoes, celery, carrots) under the roast to catch the juices and use later for gravy.

Cover and bake at 350°F oven for 2 hours until meat is done.

Remove meat to serving platter.

Remove vegetables from pan and puree in food processor and return to pan. Add to juices (drippings) from pan to thicken.

Add in sour cream and serve with roast.

POTATO STRATA

    2 tbsp butter
    ½ c onion finely diced
    3 c potatoes, sliced thin
    2 tbsp corn starch
    1 tbsp garlic, chopped
    2 ½ c chicken stock
    ½ c parmesan cheese, grated
    3 tbsp herb blend (thyme, oregano)
    ¼ c whipping cream
    Salt & Pepper to taste

~

Using a heavy bottom pot, melt butter and sauté onions and garlic together for a minute, until clear.

Stir in 2 c of chicken stock, reserving ½ c to blend with cornstarch. Add in herb blend, mix well. Bring mixture to a boil and add in cornstarch mixture to thicken.

Whisk in parmesan cheese and whipping cream until thick and smooth.

Add in potatoes, ensuring to coat the thin slices without break them. Cook over heat for five minutes.

Transfer mixture to casserole dish and bake at 350°F uncovered for an hour.

Let stand for 15-minutes to set before serving.

GINGER CARROTS

    8 med carrots
    2 tbsp butter
    2 tbsp honey
    1 tsp ginger
    ½ tsp salt
    ~

Steam carrots until just tender.

Melt butter in separate saucepan and mix in remaining ingredients and blend.

Pour over cooked carrots and serve hot.

BRAISED PEARL ONIONS WITH PEAS AND BACON

    10 oz pearl onions
    6 strips bacon, cut into small pieces
    ½ tsp salt
    ½ tsp pepper
    1 c water
    1 c frozen peas
    1 tbsp butter
    2 tsp Thyme
    ~

Braise is a low and slow cooking method to draw the sweetness from the vegetables. Very little liquid is used

Bring saucepan of water to a boil. Add onions and simmer for 2-minutes; drain and immediately immerse in large bowl of cold water to cook for 5-minutes. Using a paring knife, cut off root ends; slide off skins and discard. Set onions aside.

Fry bacon in skillet over medium-high heat until cooked but on crispy; about 6-minutes. Transfer to plate, Drain all but 2 tbsp of fat from skillet. Add onions and cook over medium-high heat, stirring often until golden; about 8-minutes. Add salt, pepper and water, scraping up browned bits from bottom of skillet.

Reduce heat to a simmer, cover and cook 15-minutes. Stir in peas, cover and cook 5-minutes more until peas are tender, but still bright green.

Just before serving stir in reserved bacon, butter and Thyme.

BAKED ONIONS

24 white pearl onions (2 c)
3 tbsp butter
1 tbsp brown sugar
1 tsp salt
¼ tsp nutmeg
6 whole cloves
Dash cayenne
Dash pepper
~

Peel onions and book in boiling water for 5 minutes. Drain. Melt butter in shallow casserole dish, stir in all ingredients, except onions and mix well. Add in onions and toss to coat.

Bask in 325 °F oven for 45 minutes or until onions are tender. Before serving remove cloves.

CHERRY CHEESECAKE

½ c butter
1 ½ c GF graham cracker crumbs
1 8-oz container cream cheese, softened
1 c sugar
1 tbsp lemon juice
1 c whipping cream
1 can cherry pie filling (check to ensure GF)

~

Crust

Melt butter and stir in GF graham cracker crumbs, press into 9x9" pan and bake at 350°F for 10-minutes. Cool.

Filling

Beat cheese, sugar and lemon juice together to dissolve sugar. In separate bowl whip whipping cream with hand blender until stiff and then fold into cheese mixture to spread over cooled crust.

Top with cherry pie filling or desired fruit of choice,

24.

Chilly Day

Ode to the biscuits, my family's favourite. Sometimes I think I make these biscuits so often that they will get sick of them, but no, as soon as they are coming out of the oven there are quick to snatch them right off the tray.

The chowder is another fast and easy meal. Hearty and filling, combined with an easy to make recipe makes this a good through the week meal idea.

~ Menu ~

Fruity Salad

Biscuits

Ham chowder

Fairy Gingerbread

FRUITY SALAD

2 c lettuce shredded
½ c fresh strawberries, sliced
½ c red grapes, halved
½ c green grapes, halved
¼ c carrots, sliced thin
¼ c red onion, chopped fine
2 tbsp feta cheese

<u>Dressing</u>
2 tsp ginger
½ lemon, squeezed, seeds removed
¼ c oil
⅛ c GF soy sauce
1 tbsp cider vinegar
1 tbsp sugar
Coarse salt and pepper to taste

~

Add all ingredients to large salad bowl and toss to mix. Drizzle with dressing just before serving

Dressing

Add all ingredients to blender and blend well for at least 1-3 minutes. Chill in fridge and shake before serving.

HAM CHOWDER

2 c diced potato
1 c onion, diced
1 c celery, finely chopped
⅓ c carrot, finely chopped
1 GF chicken bouillon cube
1 c water
1 tsp parsley flakes
¾ c frozen peas
2 ham steaks
2 c milk
1 c cheddar cheese, grated

~

Add water to saucepan, bring to a boil and add potato, onion, carrot, parsley and GF chicken bouillon cube and simmer until vegetables are tender, approximately 20 minutes. Cool and run through blender to puree. Pour back into saucepan.

Add peas, chopped ham, milk and cheese, heat stirring often. Gently simmer until heated through.

BISCUITS

    1 ¾ c GF flour
    2 tsp xanthan gum
    1 tsp soda
    1 tsp cider vinegar
    ¼ c sugar
    4 tsp baking powder
    ½ tsp salt
    ¼ c cold butter
    1 lg egg
    ⅔ c milk
    ~

Preheat oven to 425°F

In large bowl, mix GF flour, xanthan gum, sugar, baking powder and salt with butter until crumbly. Add soda to top of mixture, pour cider vinegar on top to create the fizz, mix together.

In small bowl beat egg until frothy and add milk. Pour into flour mixture and knead until just blended. Don't over blend as biscuits will become hard.

Turn out to GF floured surface and roll to desired thickness, using plastic cup, cut into large circles. Place on baking sheet and bake for 15-minutes until golden brown.

FAIRY GINGERBREAD

½ c butter
½ c sugar
1 c molasses
2 eggs
3 tsp soda
1 tsp cider vinegar
2 c GF flour
2 tsp xanthan gum
½ tsp salt
1 ½ tsp ginger
1 tsp cinnamon
1 c boiling water
½ tsp vanilla

~

Cream butter and sugar together, add eggs and beat until creamy. Add molasses and beat again. Add 1 c GF flour, xanthan gum, salt, ginger and cinnamon and mix thoroughly.

In middle of mixture, place 1 tsp of soda and cider vinegar to create reaction, mix and add remaining GF flour.

In separate bowl, add 2 tsp of soda to boiling water to create fizz; add in degrees to other mixture, top with vanilla and mix well. Add raisins, if desired.

Cook in 350°F oven until firm, about 45-minutes. Check with knife, if comes out clean, cake is done.

CARAMEL SAUCE

    1 c sugar
    1 ½ c cream
    ⅛ tsp salt
    ½ tsp vanilla
    ~

Heat iron skillet quite hot and sprinkle a small amount of sugar into the skillet to liquefy. As sugar liquefies, push to side and add more sugar until all sugar is melted to a rich amber colour. Keep stirring to prevent scorching.

Add the cream slowly (the sugar will harden) and hold at a simmering temperature continually stirring until all the caramel dissolves and the sauce is a smooth, thick consistency (from 8-10-minutes).

Add in salt and vanilla and blend well. Cool and store.

If too thick, thin with cream to desired consistency.

25.

Thanksgiving

Thanksgiving is suppose to be over the top with flavour and choice. The only challenge with this meal is getting the gravy to the right consistency. A helpful hint is to roast some side root vegetables, carrots, onion, potato right in the same pan with the turkey (not too many) then when you use the drippings to make the gravy, puree the vegetables for a natural thickener, not to mention all the added flavour!

This caramel sauce is such a hit, I have made it separately, stored in the fridge to add as a topping for ice cream for a through the week treat.

~ Menu ~

Zucchini Salad

Cranberry Sauce

Turkey

Dressing

Gravy

Creamy Mashed Potatoes

Yam Pie

Green Beans

Turnip

Apple Cake

Caramel Sauce

ZUCCHINI SALAD

    2 lg Zucchini (one yellow, one green)
    1 red onion
    12 cherry tomatoes
    1 tbsp salt
    ½ lemon
    1 tsp sugar
    1 tbsp olive oil

~

Slice zucchini and red onion into long strips. Place in bowl and sprinkle with salt. Stir to coat and set aside for 15-minutes.

The vegetables should be soft after 15-minutes. Place in sieve and rinse thoroughly to remove salt. Place on tea towel and dry completely.

Put dried vegetables in bowl; add in halved tomatoes and mix. Cut lemon in half and squeeze over vegetables, sprinkle with sugar and add olive oil. Mix well and serve fresh.

CRANBERRY SAUCE

2 c cranberries, fresh
1 med apple, peeled, cored and diced
¾ c water
1 c orange juice
¾ c sugar
Grated peel of 1 med orange
1 pkg Knox gelatine
¼ c water

~

Bring all ingredients, except gelatine to a boil, reduce heat and boil for 20-minutes.

In separate bowl, prepare gelatine according to package directions, add to cranberry mixture during last 5-minutes of cooking.

Cool and refrigerate.

TURKEY

    4 tbsp butter
    1 package of prosciutto ham, sliced think and chopped fine
    Rosemary leaves
    Thyme
    1 tbsp savoury leaves
    Salt & Pepper to taste
    Onion
    Potato
    2 carrots
    ~

Empty turkey in preparation for oven. Stuff with dressing.

Mix 3 tbsp of butter with prosciutto ham, rosemary and thyme.

Slide hand under skin of turkey to loosen. Wedge ham mixture in between the skin and meat of the turkey (don't break the skin). Once the mixture is under the skin, from the outside flatten the mixture to mould around the turkey, but remain under the skin.

Once turkey is in the pan with a small amount of liquid on the bottom, add in root vegetables to cook along side for use with the gravy.

Preheat oven to 350°F and cook according to weight

Smear remaining butter over top of turkey and season with savoury leaves, salt and pepper.

Cook according to weight

DRESSING

    3 potatoes
    1 egg
    2 tbsp butter
    ¼ finely chopped celery
    ½ c finely chopped onion
    ¼ tsp each, sage and savoury
    Thyme, Pepper and Salt to taste
    1 tbsp chopped parsley
    1 ½ c GF bread crumbs
    ~

Precook potatoes and use when cool.

In a large mixing bowl, crack egg, add potatoes and mash with butter.

Add in remaining ingredients, except bread crumbs and mix well.

Add in GF bread crumbs, mix with hands until just coated. Make into balls and place inside of turkey (if desired). Remaining stuffing can be placed inside a casserole dish and cooked separately for approximately 45-minutes.

GRAVY

Drippings and root vegetables from turkey pan
Butter
Corn starch
2 c GF chicken stock

~

In large saucepan, heat drippings. Puree vegetables. Add in butter and 1 c of GF chicken stock (if desired) to bring to a simmer. Add cornstarch as required to thicken gravy, one to two tablespoons mixed with small amount of cold water or cold stock, until clear and well blended. Pour into saucepan and whisk smooth, ensuring no lumps.

Season with salt and pepper to taste.

CREAMY MASHED POTATOES

8 potatoes
Garlic to taste (typically 1-2)
¼ c whipping cream
Large dollop of sour cream
1 tbsp butter
Chives
1 tsp dill weed

~

Peel and chop potatoes and add to large pot, cover completely with water, add in smashed garlic and bring to a boil to cook potatoes completely. Drain potatoes, mash coarsely with butter; add cream and sour cream, whip potatoes to smooth.

Stir in chives and dill weed. Serve hot.

YAM PIE

2 large yams, peeled and boiled until soft (typically 20-minutes)
¼ c brown sugar
2 tbsp butter
1 tbsp orange juice
2 tsp grated orange rind
¼ tsp cinnamon
Dash nutmeg
1 tbsp brown sugar (for top)
1 tbsp honey (for top)
Crushed pecans (optional and to taste)
~

Mash cooked yams with brown sugar, butter, orange juice, orange rind, cinnamon and nutmeg until smooth.

Transfer to casserole dish and spread evenly.

Mix brown sugar with honey and drizzle over top and sprinkle with pecans, if desired, or more grated orange rind.

GREEN BEANS

Place green beans in vegetable steamer. Bring ¼ c water to boil and steam beans for five minutes.

Drain completely, drizzle with butter and sprinkle with a touch of nutmeg

TURNIP

Turnip
¼ c brown sugar
1 tbsp butter

~

Coarsely chop and cook turnip completely in boiling water, drain when done (typically 25-minutes).

Mash turnip with butter and brown sugar.

Serve hot.

APPLE CAKE

8 med baking apples, peeled and sliced thinly
½ c sugar (to mix with sliced apples)
4 eggs
1 ½ c sugar
½ c canola oil
2 c rice flour (or flour blend of choice)
2 tsp xanthan gum
½ tsp soda
½ tsp cider vinegar
½ c orange juice
2tsp baking powder
¼ c sugar (for top of cake)
2 tbsp cinnamon (for top of cake)
2 tbsp vegetable oil (to grease baking dish

~

In a large bowl, mixed sliced apples with sugar and set aside

Preheat oven to 350°F

Mix together eggs and 1 ½ c sugar and oil and beat well.

Add in baking powder, xanthan gum and 1 c of rice flour, mix well until blended and add in orange juice.

Dollop the soda in the middle of the batter and add the cider vinegar directly on top to create a fizzle reaction, then blend well and add remaining flour.

Grease 9"x13" baking pan with remaining oil and pour in a 1/3 of the cake batter. Place apples evenly over the batter. Top apples with remaining cake batter.

Mix together sugar and cinnamon and sift evenly over top of cake.

Bake for 1 hour until golden brown. Serve warm, with ice cream, drizzled with caramel sauce.

CARAMEL SAUCE

    1 c sugar
    1 ½ c cream
    ⅛ tsp salt
    ½ tsp vanilla

~

Heat iron skillet quite hot and sprinkle a small amount of sugar into the skillet to liquefy. As sugar liquefies, push to side and add more sugar until all sugar is melted to a rich amber colour. Keep stirring to prevent scorching.

Add the cream slowly (the sugar will harden) and hold at a simmering temperature continually stirring until all the caramel dissolves and the sauce is a smooth, thick consistency (from 8-10-minutes). Add salt and vanilla and blend well. Cool and store. If too thick, thin with cream to desired consistency.

26.

Halloween

My kids have come to love 'mommy's test kitchen', which the youngest originally referred to as 'mommy's taste kitchen'. I loved it too as they would be the taste testers and if I couldn't get it by my kids, I knew the recipe had no hope. They had to like what I was cooking for them, bottom line.

The best part of this meal is the share-ability with the kids. It's ghoulish fun to have the kids get their hands in the 'guts' of the ingredients to help.

~ Menu ~

Gutsy Burgers

Broken Fingers

Dirty Ghosts

Oozing Apple Lanterns

Brown Sugar Fudge

GUTSY BURGERS

    1 lb burger
    Cheddar cheese cut into six 1" cubes
    ¼ c GF salsa
    Salt & pepper to taste
    6 lg romaine lettuce leaves
    ~

Form burger patty and break in half, making thin patty. Top with cheese cube and tsp of salsa, top with another thin patty, kneading the edges completely together to prevent leakage.

Place on grate on top of baking sheet to cook in 400°F oven for 40-minutes until desired doneness.

Serve wrapped in romaine lettuce leaf.

BROKEN FINGERS

    6 potatoes, cut into thin wedges
    2 tbsp oil
    Salt and pepper to taste
    Ketchup to garnish
    ~

Drizzle oil over cut potato wedges and place in single layer on cooking sheet.

Sprinkle with salt and pepper.

Cook in 400°F oven for 25-30-minutes until tender and golden brown.

Dip some ends in ketchup to garnish, break others to arrange on plate.

DIRTY GHOSTS

1 bag large marshmallows
3 Aero chocolate bars
2 tbsp whipping cream
1 tsp cinnamon

~

Melt Aero bars on low heat with whipping cream and cinnamon.

Dip tops of marshmallows in chocolate, turn to stand on undipped side letting the chocolate slide down the sides.

Place on cookie sheet in fridge to cool completely.

Serve at room temperature

OOZING APPLE LANTERNS

5 med apples
Fruit of filling of choice (caramel / butterscotch / chocolate)

~

Peel apples and core top part of apples, on four of the apples, leaving a bottom and saving the top to serve as a 'hat'. Use the fifth apple for decorating.

Cut lantern faces in apples, add legs, arms to decorate as desired.

Fill apples with desired filling and bake in 350°F oven for 40-minutes until apples are soft.

Serve topped with more filling and ice cream.

BROWN SUGAR FUDGE

    3 c brown sugar
    1 c evaporated milk
    1 tbsp corn syrup
    1 tsp vanilla
    3 tbsp butter

~

In medium saucepan combine brown sugar with evaporated milk and corn syrup, bring to a boil, stirring constantly.

Continue boiling, stirring frequently to soft ball stage when candy thermometer reads 234 - 238°F.

Remove from heat and add vanilla and butter; do not stir.

Let cool about 25-minutes then beat with wooden spoon until fudge begins to thicken.

Continue to stir for a few more minutes until fudge begins to lose its gloss, but is not too thick.

Spread on greased pie plate.

Score when set and cut into squares when firm.

27.

Nice 'n Easy

~ Menu ~

Roasted Portabella Salad

Coconut Shrimp Curry

Coconut Ginger Rice

GF Oatmeal Cookies

ROASTED PORTABELLA SALAD

½ c olive oil
¼ c cider vinegar
1 tsp thyme
4 portabella mushroom caps, brushed, cleaned and stems removed
1 c grape tomatoes, halved
4 c spinach
½ c parmesan cheese
Dash salt & pepper

~

In bowl, whisk together 3 tbsp oil with vinegar and thyme and marinade mushroom caps to coat and set aside.

Toss tomatoes in marinade and set aside.

Heat oven to 400°F.

On baking sheet, line mushroom caps on one side and tomatoes on the other. Roast in oven for 12 minutes.

Let cool slightly before slicing mushrooms.

In salad bowl, toss spinach, parmesan with remaining oil, salt and pepper. Spread spinach on serving platter and top with tomatoes and mushrooms.

Just before serving drizzle with remaining marinade.

COCONUT SHRIMP CURRY

    1 tsp oil
    2 tsp curry
    2 tsp ginger
    ½ onion, sliced thin
    ½ c coconut milk
    2 c frozen Asian vegetables
    Jumbo shrimp
    ~

Heat oil over medium high heat in large skillet and add curry and ginger until fragrant, about 30-seconds.

Add onion and cook 2 minutes until clear.

Add coconut milk to mix thoroughly, then the vegetables and shrimp.

Heat through about 15-minutes.

COCONUT GINGER RICE

    2 tbsp oil
    2 tbsp ginger, fresh grated
    1 tbsp orange rind, grated
    1 ½ c rice (long grain)
    1 ½ c water
    1 c coconut milk
    4 green onions, chopped
    1 tsp salt
    ¼ tsp pepper

~

Heat oil in saucepan with lid, add ginger and cook, stirring for 2 minutes, add rice and cook another minute until it crackles. Add water, coconut milk, green onion, orange rind, salt and pepper, stirring well.

Reduce heat to low and cook for 20-30-minutes until rice is cooked through.

Fluff before serving.

GF OATMEAL COOKIES

½ c butter, softened (room temperature)
1 c brown sugar, packed
1 lg egg
1 tsp vanilla
1c GF flour
1 tsp xanthan gum
1 c GF oats
1 tsp soda
1 tsp cider vinegar
¼ tsp salt
1 c GF chocolate chips
OR
½ c raisins

~

Preheat oven to 350°F.

Add butter, brown sugar, egg and vanilla to mixing bowl and beat until smooth. Add GF flour, xanthan gum and salt to stir into mixture. Add in GF oats to mix well.

Add soda, then cider vinegar on top to create the fizz, blend well. Add remaining ingredients until well mixed.

Form dough into tbsp sized balls and place on cookie sheet and bake for 10-12-minutes.

28.

Football

Certainly a meal that takes less time than most and will be sure to please the sports lover with the football shaped chicken to match the occasion.

With the potato wedges and coleslaw, they may forget they're at home and not at the pub.

~ Menu ~

Prosciutto wrapped Chicken

Buddy burgers

Coconut coleslaw

Potato wedges

Chocolate Chip Cookies

PROSCIUTTO WRAPPED CHICKEN

4 lg chicken breast
2 pkg prosciutto ham
½ container feta cheese, sliced in lengths
2 lg peppers, thickly sliced
~

Preheat oven to 350°F.

Cut chicken into thick wedge like pieces, just enough to fill the strip of prosciutto.

Line a strip of pepper and feta beside chick and wrap in prosciutto tightly.

Lay along cookie sheet and bake for 35-40 minutes until chicken is cooked through.

BUDDY BURGERS

½ c ketchup
2 tbsp GF soy sauce
1 tbsp chilli powder
1 lb burger
1 onion, minced
½ c cheddar cheese, shredded
2 tbsp corn starch
~

In mixing bowl, combine all ingredients and shape into patties.

Grill on barbeque until done.

POTATO WEDGES

    4 lg potatoes, peeled and sliced thickly
    1 tsp paprika
    ½ tsp chilli powder
    ½ tsp curry powder
    1 tsp salt
    ½ tsp pepper
    ~

Mix spices together in large ziplock bag. Add rinsed potato wedges, a few at a time to coat.

Lay on single layer on cooking sheet and bake in 350°F oven for 35-40-minutes until tender.

COCONUT COLESLAW

    ½ c sour cream
    ½ c mayonnaise
    1 tsp lemon juice
    1 tsp salt
    ¼ tsp paprika
    ¼ tsp curry powder
    1 c coconut
    4 c cabbage, shredded
    2 tbsp green onion, minced
    ~

Mix together first 6 ingredients, until well blended, stir in coconut and let stand ½ hour.

Add cabbage and green onion and let stand another 15-minutes before serving.

CHOCOLATE CHIP COOKIES

1 ½ c GF flour
1 ½ tsp xanthan gum
1 tsp soda
1 tsp cider vinegar
½ tsp salt
½ c butter
¼ c brown sugar
½ c white sugar
1 ½ tsp vanilla
1 egg, beaten
1 tsp cream cheese
1 c GF chocolate chips

~

Cream butter and sugars together, add in cream cheese, eggs and vanilla and blend well. Mix in flour and salt until well blended. Top with soda and then the cider to create the fizz and then mix well.

Toss in chocolate chips until mixed through and drop by the spoonful onto greased cookie sheet.

Bake in 350°F oven for 10-15-minutes.

29.

Remembrance Day

The biscuit lips is just an alternate version of the basic biscuit, while the oven-baked rice is a nice make ahead dish that can be used as a through the week meal by lining the casserole with pork chops and ladling the rice on top to bake. It's a complete meal all in one pan.

The challenge to this meal is the strudel. As an alternate, if you have a tough time with pastry dough as many do, you can purchase premade gluten-free pie shells and roll to thin the crust out to use for this recipe.

~ Menu ~

Cranberry Spinach Salad

Biscuit Lips

Cinnamon Honey Butter

Sweet Chilli Pork Lettuce Wraps

Oven Baked Rice

Asparagus with Cashew Butter

Apple Strudel with Vanilla Sauce

CRANBERRY SPINACH SALAD

1 sm can mandarin oranges, drained
1 pkg spinach, torn
½ c craisins
½ c red onion, sliced thin
<u>Dressing</u>:
4 slices bacon, cooked crisp, crumbled
½ c honey
½ c lime juice
2 tbsp Dijon mustard

~

Toss mandarin's, craisins, spinach, and onion together in salad bowl.

<u>Dressing</u>:

Mix all ingredients together for dressing until well blended.

Heat for 1 minute in microwave, pour over salad and toss to coat.

BISCUIT LIPS

2 c GF flour
2 tsp xanthan gum
2 tsp soda
2 tsp cider vinegar
4 tsp baking powder
2 tbsp sugar
1 tsp salt
½ c butter
¾ c milk
Butter to spread

~

Mix GF flour, xanthan gum, sugar, salt and baking powder together. Cut in butter and mix until crumbly. Add soda and then cider vinegar on top to create fizz, add in milk and stir until just mixed.

Using GF flour, flour working surface and knead dough about 10 times before spreading dough to ¼" thick and cutting into 2 ¾" circles.

Cut through centre of circle with sharp knife to barely score the surface and spread with butter, fold dough over (butter side together) and press the edges together.

Arrange on greased baking pan and bake at 425°F oven for 8-10-minutes, until golden brown.

CINNAMON HONEY BUTTER

¼ c butter, softened
3 tbsp honey
¼ tsp cinnamon
Dash salt

~

Combine all ingredients together until smooth and serve at room temperature.

SWEET CHILLI PORK LETTUCE WRAPS

1 lb left over pork tenderloin, thinly sliced
1 tsp soda
1 tsp GF soy sauce
1 tbsp oil, divided
1 tbsp ginger
8 mushrooms, sliced
2 c red pepper, sliced
4 green onions, sliced thin
1 c GF sweet chilli sauce (most are)
¼ c water
1 lg head lettuce, iceberg

~

In large bowl combine soda, GF soy sauce, and pork, set aside to marinade for 5-minutes.

In large skillet heat 1 tsp oil over medium-high heat, add in pork and cook about 3-minutes. Transfer to plate and set aside.

Add remaining oil to cook ginger, mushrooms and red peppers until softened, about 3-minutes. Add pork, green onion, sweet chilli sauce and water and cook about 4-minutes.

Spoon mixture onto lettuce leaves, roll and serve with rice.

OVEN BAKED RICE

    1 c long grain rice
    2 c water
    3 tbsp butter
    2 tsp parsley
    ¼ tsp salt
    ¼ tsp pepper
    ~

Mix all ingredients together in casserole dish.

Cover and bake in 350°F oven for 45-minutes.

Fluff with fork before serving.

ASPARAGUS WITH CASHEW BUTTER

    Fresh asparagus
    ¼ c butter
    2 tsp lemon juice
    ¼ tsp marjoram
    ¼ cashews, uncoated
    ~

Cook asparagus in steamer for 10-minutes, drain.

In saucepan melt butter, add lemon juice, marjoram and cashews, simmer over low heat for 2 minutes. Pour over asparagus and serve.

APPLE STRUDEL WITH VANILLA SAUCE

<u>Strudel</u>
1 c GF flour
1 tsp xanthan gum
1 tsp soda
1 tsp cider vinegar
½ tsp salt
1 lg egg yolk
¼ c water, warm
2 tsp oil
4 med apples, peeled, cored and sliced
¼ c raisins
¼ c sugar
½ tsp cinnamon
¼ c butter, melted, divided

<u>Vanilla Sauce</u>
3 lg egg yolks
½ c sugar
1 c heavy cream
1 c milk
1 tsp vanilla

~

Mix together GF flour, xanthan gum, and salt with mixer, slowly add egg yolk, warm water, oil and mix. Add soda, then the cider vinegar to create fizz and mix well.

Remove dough from bowl, spread with oil and place in covered container in fridge overnight. Remove dough from fridge, preheat oven to 400°F, and lightly grease pan; set aside.

Wipe excess oil from dough, place on working surface, clean, lint-free towel and gently pull dough with hands until paper-thin about 16"x14".

Stir together sliced apples and raisins in large bowl.

Spread apples and raisins along long edge of dough closest to you, forming a 3" border.

In small bowl, mix together sugar and cinnamon to sprinkle over apples.

With pastry brush, brush remaining exposed dough with melted butter. Using the towel on the side where the apple mixture is, roll the dough to the other end, making sure that the apple mixture inside remains even. Brush outside of dough with remaining butter.

Transfer strudel to prepared pan and bake for 25-30-minutes until golden brown.

<u>Vanilla Sauce</u>

Beat together egg yolks and sugar for about 5-minutes until thick and lemony coloured. Heat heavy cream and milk over medium high heat to scald; remove from heat and allow to cool slightly. With mixer on low speed, pour the milk mixture into the yolk mixture, return entire mixture to saucepan and heat, stirring constantly over low heat until thickened and coats back of spoon.

Transfer to bowl and let cool. Add in vanilla and stir.

30.

Company's Coming

I remember first having Mulligatawny soup at my neighbour Clara's house and wow, such filling, flavourful soup with apples! With some slight modifications, it is the same flavourful soup Gluten-free.

The Quick Pudding is just as the name implies, very quick and easy to make. Another desert for the unexpected guest where you need to dress up an every day meal.

~ Menu ~

Spinach Salad

Mulligatawny Soup

Maple Ginger Pork Chops

Parmesan Potatoes

Curried Carrots

Quick Pudding

SPINACH SALAD

1 pkg spinach, fresh, torn
1 apple, peeled and chopped
4 slices bacon, crispy and crumbled
2 eggs, boiled and sliced
½ c cheddar cheese, shredded

Dressing:
1 clove garlic, minced
6 tbsp oil
2 tbsp cider vinegar
1 tsp sugar
1 tsp dry mustard
1 tsp salt
½ tsp pepper

~

In salad bowl, toss together spinach, apples, bacon. Toss with dressing to coat. Arrange boiled egg slices on top neatly and sprinkle with cheddar cheese.

Dressing:

Mix together all ingredients until well blended.

MULLIGATAWNY SOUP

2 lbs chicken, cut in pieces
4 c water
¼ tsp salt
1 tbsp butter
1 onion, chopped, fine
½ tsp curry powder
2 tbsp corn starch
4 tbsp water
1 tsp sugar
2 apples, peeled, cored and diced
2 green peppers, chopped
¼ c celery, chopped
2 carrots, chopped
2 cloves
¼ tsp nutmeg
Dash pepper
¼ c whipping cream

~

Precook chicken in 350°F oven until done.

In large cooking pot, melt butter and add onion and sauté 1 minute. Add in apples and sauté an additional 5 minutes until clear. Add curry, sugar and stir thoroughly. Add in water and salt and bring to a boil. Reduce to a simmer and add in vegetables and remaining spices. Simmer for 30 minutes until vegetables are tender.

Puree soup in blender, return to pot, add cooked chicken and whipping cream, stir thoroughly, heating through and serve hot.

As an alternative, place ½ c of cooked rice in each bowl and serve soup on top.

MAPLE GINGER PORK CHOPS

    6 pork chops
    1 c orange juice
    1 tsp Dijon mustard
    1 tsp grated fresh ginger root
    ¼ c maple syrup
    ½ tsp salt
    ¼ tsp pepper
    2 tsp cornstarch
    ~

In skillet fry pork chops until near done.

In a small bowl, combine remaining ingredients and stir until well blended.

When pork is near to cooked, pour syrup mixture over the top and simmer until fully cooked.

PARMESAN POTATOES

    4 med potatoes
    ½ c butter
    ¼ c parmesan cheese
    1 egg slightly beaten
    ~

Peel and cut potatoes into ½" thick slices. Melt ¼ c butter in pan. Dip potato slices in egg and then coat in parmesan cheese.

Place in pan in layers.

Melt remaining butter and drizzle over potatoes.

Bake in 350°F oven for 45-50-minutes

CURRIED CARROTS

4 med carrots, peeled and sliced and cooked
1 tbsp butter
⅓ c onion, minced
1 tsp cornstarch
1 tbsp curry powder
Dash pepper
1 c water

~

Melt butter in pan to sauté onions until soft 2-minutes.

Add water, curry powder and pepper to onions and bring to boil.

Mix cornstarch with small amount of water until smooth. Add to onions until blended, smooth and thickened.

Pour over carrots and serve.

QUICK PUDDING

    1 c GF flour
    1 tsp xanthan gum
    ½ tsp soda
    ½ tsp cider vinegar
    2 tbsp butter
    2 tsp baking powder
    ¼ tsp salt
    ⅓ c raisins
    ½ c milk
    1 ¾ c water, boiled
    ½ tsp cinnamon
    1 tsp vanilla
    ⅔ c brown sugar

~

In mixing bowl, stir together, GF flour, xanthan gum, butter, baking powder, salt and raisins. Add soda and cider vinegar on top to create fizz and mix well, adding in milk. Pour into greased casserole dish, smooth top.

In same bowl, combine, water, cinnamon, vanilla and brown sugar together, pour over batter, do not stir.

Bake in 350°F oven for 30 minutes.

31.

Christmas Eve

The Christmas meal is so closely related to the same menu as Thanksgiving in our house I wanted to shake it up with some samples of what we do during the holidays.

We keep the night before as easy as possible, ensure we have something fresh baked for Santa. Many times the Christmas Cake, though made Christmas Eve is served Christmas day.

~ Menu ~

Spiced Apple Cider

Ham rolls

Sheppard's Pie

Shortbread Cookies

Gingerbread People

Christmas Cake

SPICED APPLE CIDER

    1 l apple juice
    1 l orange juice
    1 c lemon juice, fresh squeezed
    ½ c honey
    4 cinnamon sticks, broken
    12 cloves, whole
    12 allspice
    ~

Combine all ingredients in a large pot and bring to boil. Reduce heat and simmer for 10-minutes until hot and fragrant.

Remove spices with slotted spoon before pouring into mugs for serving.

HAM ROLLS

    Prepared mustard
    6 cooked deli ham slices
    6 cheddar cheese slices
    2 tbsp butter, melted
    ~

Spread mustard lightly along ham slice, top with cheese, roll to secure and hold together with toothpick.

Brush with melted butter and place cook in 350°F oven for 10-15-minutes.

Cut into pieces to serve

SHEPPARD'S PIE

1 lb burger
1 tsp oil
1 med onion, minced
1 med carrot, sliced
4 potatoes, peeled and sliced
1 clove garlic, minced
1 GF bouillon cube
2 tbsp cornstarch
1 c water

~

In separate pots, boil potatoes and carrot until done, typically 20-minutes. When done, mash potatoes until fluffy. Drain carrots and coarsely mash.

In frying pan, add oil, garlic and onion and sauté for 2 minutes or until onion is clear. Add in burger and scramble, when just about done, add in GF bouillon cube.

Add cornstarch to small amount of water and stir until clear. Add water to burger and bring to a boil. Add in cornstarch mixture to thicken.

Transfer meat to greased casserole dish, layer with carrots and then potatoes on top.

Cook in 350°F oven for 35-minutes until bubbly.

GINGERBREAD PEOPLE

2 c GF flour
2 tsp xanthan gum
1 tsp soda
1 tsp cider vinegar
½ tsp salt
½ tsp baking powder
1 tsp ginger
1 tsp cloves, ground
1 ½ tsp cinnamon
½ tsp nutmeg
½ c butter, softened
½ c sugar
½ c molasses
1 egg yolk

~

Sift together GF flour, xanthan gum, baking powder, ground cloves, cinnamon and nutmeg. Blend together butter, sugar and molasses until creamy. Add egg yolk and blend well. Stir into flour mixture. Add soda and top with cider vinegar to fizz, stir well.

On lightly floured surface, roll out dough to about ¼" thick. With floured cutters, cut into gingerbread people; place on ungreased cookie sheet and back in 350°F oven for 8-10-minutes or until done.

Cool and decorate as desired.

CLASSIC SHORTBREAD

    2 c GF flour
    2 tsp xanthan gum
    1 c butter
    ½ c sugar
    1 tsp vanilla
    1 tsp milk
    ~

Mix all ingredients together to form a ball.

Roll with rolling pin on lightly GF floured surface to desired thickness, typically ½" and cut into desired shapes.

Cook in 400°F oven for 10-15-minutes until golden brown.

CHRISTMAS CAKE

    1 c butter
    1 8 oz container cream cheese
    1 ½ c sugar
    4 eggs
    1 tsp vanilla
    1 tsp lemon extract
    1 tsp almond extract
    ½ tsp salt
    1 ½ tsp baking powder
    1 ¾ c GF flour
    1 ½ tsp xanthan gum
    1 tsp soda
    1 tsp cider vinegar
    1 ½ c red & green cherries, chopped
    ¼ c GF flour

~

Preheat oven to 350°F

Mix butter, cream cheese and sugar until smooth. Add to mixture, eggs, vanilla, lemon extract and almond extract and blend until smooth. Add salt, baking powder, xanthan gum and GF flour to mixture and blend. Top with soda and cider vinegar to create fizz, mix well.

Mix drained cherries with GF flour in separate bowl and then add to wet mixture.

Transfer batter into well greased baking dish and bake for 1 hour 20-minutes, until knife inserted comes out clean.

32.

Christmas Brunch

Another thank you to Clara for this menu. Ever since she introduced us to this Christmas morning sugar rush, it has become a tradition. It has been modified from the original, of course, but still a huge hit.

~ Menu ~

Land of Nod cinnamon rolls with cream cheese icing

Egg sandwiches

Omelette Casserole

Poached Fruit

LAND OF NOD CINNAMON ROLLS WITH CREAM CHEESE ICING

For dough setting on a bread maker

1 ⅔ c water, luke warm

2 tbsp powdered milk

2 tbsp butter

2 tbsp sugar

2 tsp salt

4 c GF flour

4 tsp xanthan gum

2 tsp soda

2 tsp cinder vinegar

1 ½ tsp yeast

<u>Sauce</u>

¼ c brown sugar, packed

¾ c raisins

2 tbsp cinnamon

½ c butter

<u>Icing</u>

¾ c cream cheese, room temperature

½ c butter, room temperature

1 tsp vanilla

1 c icing sugar (add more if icing is too thin)

~

Place all ingredients for dough in the bread maker in order, except soda and cider vinegar. Allow bread maker to mix all ingredients and about ½ hour into process, add soda and cider vinegar.

Dough will be sticky coming out of bread maker. Take another cup of GF flour and use to form into balls.

Sauce

Mix all ingredients together until smooth. Pour over dough balls, ensuring each ball is coated with sauce and cook in 350°F oven for 25-minutes

Roll dough balls into sauce and place in well greased, round bunt pa.

Leave dough to raise (overnight in fridge preferable) and cook 20-25-minutes Christmas morning.

Icing

Beat all ingredients together until smooth.

When buns are cooked and cooled slightly, turn out onto serving tray and drizzle icing over cooked buns and serve hot.

EGG SANDWICHES
6 hard boiled eggs
3 tbsp celery, finely diced
½ tsp salt
½ tsp parsley
¼ tsp onion, minced
¼ c mayonnaise
~
Mix all ingredients together and spread over Udi GF bread, topped with lettuce.

OMELETTE CASSEROLE

6 bacon slices, fried and drained of grease
1 tbsp butter
1 lb mushrooms, fresh, sliced
4 green onion, sliced
8 eggs
1 c milk
½ tsp salt
¼ tsp pepper
2 ½ c cheddar cheese

~

Sauté mushrooms and onion in butter, in frying pan.

Beat eggs in bowl until frothy, mix in milk, salt, pepper and cheese. Crumble bacon and add along with mushrooms and onions and mix well. Pour into casserole dish and bake in 350°F oven, uncovered for 40 minutes until set.

POACHED FRUIT

1 bottle vin santo (Tuscan dessert wine)
2 c water
1 ½ c sugar
1 lg cinnamon stick
6 whole cloves
1 vanilla bean
Zest of 1 orange
Zest of 1 lemon
10 pears, whole
1 ½ c lg dried figs
1 ½ c lg dried apricots
¾ c lg dried prunes

~

Add vin santo, sugar, cinnamon, cloves, vanilla bean and zests in large, shallow saucepan with water. Bring to a boil, reduce heat to low and simmer for 10-minutes.

Peel the pears, leaving stems intact and scoop out seeds from bottom using an apple corer. Lay half the pears on their sides in the poaching liquid and simmer for 20-minutes, carefully turning the pears once with a spoon. Remove from liquid with a slotted spoon.

Repeat the poaching of the remaining pears in the same liquid. Snip off the hard stems from the figs, adding the figs, apricots, prunes and first batch of pears and simmer for 5-10-minutes more until fruit is tender.

Chill the mixture, removing the cinnamon, cloves and vanilla bean before serving.

33.

Boxing Day

After all the heavy eating during the holiday's a nice menu idea to use up the left overs and eat a little lighter.

Pick and choose what works for you, but keep it easy.

~ Menu ~

Green Tea Latte

Stuffed Peppers

Turkey Bake

Potato Deluxe

Squash and Apple Saute

Ice Cream with Chocolate Fudge Sauce

GF Rice Crispy Squares

GREEN TEA LATTE

    4 c boiling water
    4 green tea bags
    ½ c condensed milk
    ~

Pour boiling water over tea bags and let sit for 5 minutes. Remove tea bags and add milk.

Whisk until smooth and serve hot.

STUFFED PEPPERS

    4 lg peppers
    1 tbsp oil
    1 onion, minced
    1 clove garlic, minced
    ¾ lbs burger
    1 ½ c tomato sauce
    1 tbsp GF Worcestershire sauce
    ½ tsp salt
    1 tbsp water
    Dash pepper
    2 tbsp corn starch
    ~

Slice stem ends off peppers, remove core and seeds.

Add oil to sauce pan with garlic and onion and cook until soft, about 2-minutes. Add burger and cook until done. Add tomato sauce, GF Worcestershire sauce, salt and pepper and stir until blended and bubbly.

Mix cornstarch with water until smooth and add to mixture to thicken. Reduce heat and use mixture to fill peppers.

Cook in 350°F oven for 35-minutes.

Serve hot.

TURKEY CASSEROLE

2 c left over turkey
1 bag frozen mixed vegetables
1 c GF chicken stock
1 tbsp cornstarch
1 c mayonnaise
1 tsp lemon juice
1 tsp curry powder
2 c cheddar cheese, shredded

~

Layer frozen mixed vegetables on bottom of greased casserole dish. Top with left over turkey.

In small bowl mix GF chicken stock, cornstarch, mayonnaise, lemon juice, curry powder together until well blended. Pour over turkey and top with cheese.

Cook in 350°F oven for 40-minutes until bubbly.

POTATO DELUXE

5 c cooked potatoes, diced into squares
1 onion, diced
1 c GF chicken stock
1 tbsp cornstarch
1 sm container sour cream
½ c butter
1 c cheddar cheese, grated
Salt & Pepper to taste
1 green onion, diced

~

In bowl, mix together GF chicken stock, sour cream and cornstarch until well blended. Toss potatoes, onion, salt and pepper together. Pour sauce over potatoes to mix well. Turn into casserole dish and sprinkle with cheese.

Cook in 350°F oven for 1 hour.

SQUASH AND APPLE SAUTE

    2 sweet baby dumpling squash
    2 tbsp butter
    2 lg apples, cored and chopped
    1 leek, sliced, white part only
    2 tbsp white wine
    ¼ tsp cinnamon
    Dash pepper
    Dash nutmeg

~

Halve squashes; cook, covered in small amount of boiling water about 15-minutes.

Melt butter in large skillet, add apples, leek slices and sauté for 5-minutes.

Add wine and spices and cook an additional 3-minutes.

Carefully scoop out squash and mash; add to skillet and blend with apple mixture.

Spoon mixture into squash shells and serve immediately.

ICE CREAM WITH CHOCOLATE FUDGE SAUCE

½ c cocoa powder
1 c sugar
1 c light corn syrup
½ c light cream
3 tbsp butter
¼ tsp salt
1 tsp vanilla

~

Combine all ingredients, except vanilla in saucepan and boil for 5-minutes.

Remove from heat and stir in vanilla.

Makes about 2 cups.

Serve over ice cream.

GF RICE CRISPY SQUARES

¼ c butter
1 pkg marshmallows
6 c GF rice cereal (Kinnikinnick brand)
½ tsp vanilla

~

In large pot melt butter and add marshmallows until melted.

Stir in vanilla and then add cereal until well coated.

Press into large shallow casserole pan.

34.

Dinner with the Mob

An all-time favourite movie – the Godfather – and we always seem to watch the three of them at some point over the holiday's while recouping from the many large meals just relaxing. Why not take a page from the many scenes of that book and create a meal to accompany the entertainment.

The interesting thing I learned from putting this meal together is the stand-alone quality and versatility of all of these dishes.

~ *Menu* ~

Sausage & Peppers

Roasted Peppers

Meatballs

Clemenza Sauce

Spaghetti

Pasta Fagiole

Sicilian Meatloaf

Custard Cream Gelato

SAUSAGE & PEPPERS

    1-2 lg Freyby sausages, cut in 1"-2" pieces
    2 red peppers, cut into 1" pieces
    2 green peppers, cut into 1" pieces
    3 onions, quartered

~

Put all ingredients into a baking dish, cover and bake in 350°F oven for 1 hour.

Take the cover off and bake on 400°F oven for about 30 minutes until the sausage begins to brown.

Transfer to serving dish.

ROASTED PEPPERS

Take a couple of bell peppers. Wash them well. Turn the oven on high and cook them, quickly, turning them on all sides until they turn black.

Take them out and peel the burnt skin off, cut them, deseed them, and drizzle a little olive oil over them.

MEAT BALLS

    1 lb burger
    1 tbsp cornstarch
    ½ tsp salt
    1 tsp oregano
    1 tsp Italian spices

~

In large bowl, mix all ingredients together.

Form meat into small teaspoon sized balls, lay on baking dish and cook in 350°F oven for 25-30-minutes.

CLEMENZA SAUCE

2 cloves garlic, minced
1 sm onion, diced
1 sm red pepper, diced
2 tbsp olive oil
2 sun dried tomatoes, stored in oil, diced
1 sm can tomato paste
1 sm can tomato sauce
1 tsp sugar
½ tsp salt
1 tsp oregano
1 tsp basil

~

Add oil to saucepan, toss in garlic and onion and sauté a couple of minutes until garlic is golden.

Add in sun dried tomatoes with little bit of the oil from the tomatoes. Cook an additional 2 minutes.

Stir in tomato sauce, mix well and then the tomato paste, sugar, salt and oregano. Mix well and simmer until ready to serve.

As an option, add in some red wine for flavour.

Add meatballs to sauce to coat and serve with pasta

GF SPAGHETTI PASTA

To cook pasta fill a large pot three quarts full of boiling water, keep it on a high heat and pour the pasta in, season the water with salt to taste and cook in the water till Al Dente (9-12 minutes), keep on trying the pasta throughout cooking until satisfied with its texture, it should not be too hard and firm, but it shouldn't be soft and mushy.

PASTA FAGIOLE

2 tbsp olive oil
1 medium onion, diced fine
5 cloves garlic, chopped
1 c carrots, diced
1 c celery, diced
6 oz. can tomato paste
1 lb. GF pasta, cooked al dente
1 cube GF chicken bouillon
2 bay leaves
2 cans cooked pink beans
2 quarts GF chicken stock
Salt and Pepper to taste.

~

In large skillet, heat olive oil to sauté onions, carrots & celery with bay leaves and garlic for 10 minutes, until vegetables are soft.

Add tomato paste and cook 5 minutes more.

Add ½ of the stock. Heat through.

Add 1 can of beans, pureed in blender and 1 can of whole beans.

Add cooked pasta, season with bouillon and salt & pepper.

Adjust to desired thickness with extra stock.

SICILIAN MEATLOAF

½ tbsp olive oil
1 lb ground burger
1 tsp Italian spices
3 tbsp GF breadcrumbs
½ lg onion, diced fine
1 egg, slightly beaten
1 tsp parsley
3 tbsp parmesan cheese, grated
1 sm can tomato sauce (reserve half for top)
½ tsp GF Worcestershire sauce
¼ tsp pepper
½ tsp salt
1 egg, hard boiled, cooled, peeled and cut in half lengthwise
1 pkg sliced prosciutto
Provolone cheese, cut in 1 ½" strips

~

Preheat oven to 350°F

Lightly coat a loaf pan with olive oil. In a large bowl, combine all ingredients except the reserved tomato sauce, hard boiled egg, prosciutto and provolone, and mix well (this is done easily with your hands). The mixture should hold together but not be hard.

Adjust the consistency if needed by adding either GF bread crumbs or tomato sauce. Divide mixture in half. Put one half of meatloaf mixture into the prepared pan, shaping to fit and flattening slightly.

Cover with slices of prosciutto, and place the egg halves in a row horizontally on top of the prosciutto, cut side up.

Layer the provolone strips over the egg halves and extend cheese to cover almost to the edges of the meatloaf.

Top with the remaining half of meatloaf mixture and seal halves together, covering the filling.

Top with remaining tomato sauce.

Bake 30 minutes.

CUSTARD CREAM GELATO

    6 c milk (whole or 2%)
    1 ½ c sugar
    12 egg yolks, beaten
    1 tbsp grated orange or lemon peel
    ~

In a large saucepan combined egg yolks, 3 cups of milk and sugar.

Cook and whisk over very low heat until mixture sticks to the metal utensil. Be very careful not to cook the eggs.

Remove from heat and gradually mix in the remaining 3 cups of milk and grated peel. Cover and chill in the refrigerator overnight or place the saucepan in an ice bath until completely chilled.

This recipe makes around 2 to 3 quarts of gelato.

These gelato recipes can be adjusted to make a smaller portion.

Made in the USA
Charleston, SC
31 July 2013